RUSTING
TOYS

The story of eight children
and the parents who abused them.

DR. DALE DOUGLAS

TOUCH
PUBLISHING

Published by Touch Publishing
P.O. Box 180303
Arlington, Texas 76096 U.S.A.
www.TouchPublishingServices.com

Cover design by Touch Publishing
Edited by Kimberly Soesbee
Author photo by David Soesbee

Library of Congress Control Number: 2015955346

Douglas, Dr. Dale
      Rusting Toys / Dr. Dale Douglas
p. cm.

Printed in the United States of America

Connect with the author: www.DrDaleDouglas.com

* Back cover statistics from Childhelp.org, Phoenix, Arizona

TABLE OF CONTENTS

INTRODUCTION

I must confess that I went to Mr. Webster to seek out the definition of certain words that recur with each turn of the page in this book. However, I already had definitions in mind based on my life experiences. I feel it is important for you to have them, too, as a basis for reading this story.

- Abuse: improper or excessive use or treatment.
- Beating: an act of striking with repeated blows so as to injure or damage.
- Evil: morally reprehensible or arising from actual or imputed bad character or conduct or causing harm.
- Life: the quality that distinguishes a vital and functional being from a dead body.
- Lost: ruined or destroyed physically or morally or beyond reach or attainment.
- Neglect: to leave undone or unattended or insufficient attention to something that merits attention.
- Parent: a person who brings up or cares for another.
- Rust: corrosive or injurious influence or effect or causing to be of little or no worth.
- Survival: the act or fact of living
- Trust: to place confidence in or rely on as the truth or as being confident in as not to cause harm.

You may find this a strange combination of words, but it is my hope that by the time you finish this book, you will appreciate the extra effort given to providing you with these meanings.

There are 4.3 births in this world every second, which equates to about 353,000 babies per day worldwide. Statistically, 734 male babies that are born each day will die before reaching age one. In the United States alone, 337 children between the ages of 1 and 4 will die because of homicide. In the United States, 386 children between the ages of 10 and 14 will take their own lives. Why would I bring all this up?

When a child is born, the world does not find it unreasonable to expect the people who bring him or her into the world to take care of all the child's needs including love, shelter, safety, food, clothing, medical care, trust, warmth in cold, cool in heat, faith needs, stability, and security. Sometimes this just doesn't happen.

This story is about the eight children born to a couple who married in the 1940s and the life journey of each. Further, this is the true story about eight children who were abused and neglected as infants, children, pre-teens, teens, and young adults and describes how each one's stages in life were dictated by what he or she heard, felt, thought, and imagined through the words and actions or lack of actions by this couple, other family, neighbors, schoolmates, church members, clergy, and others. By the end of this book, the list of words that I have provided may take on different meanings or definitions for you.

Some of you will be angered, some will be sad, some will be in disbelief, some will be shocked, some will feel pity, and some will carry other feelings, but all will come to an understanding that Jesus Christ has to play a part in every human being's life if life is going to have any kind of meaning. There is no other meaning for Jesus Christ other than love. If you doubt it, read carefully these pages.

It is not my intention to shine light on the sins of my brothers and sisters, but I have no problem sharing my own. This is who I am. However, it is difficult to discuss each child's struggles through life without mentioning, at least in part, some of the sins that have resulted from just trying to survive life. Yes, that is correct. We survived life; we didn't live it.

You will discover as never before how the sins of the father (or mother) are passed down from generation to generation. You will also discover that the only way that this vicious circle can ever be broken is through the blood of Jesus Christ.

Keep in mind that biological parents are not the only ones who take an active part in raising a child. In addition to people, places and experiences have a large influence on how a child will grow and what he or she will grow into.

Finally, it is my most fervent desire that you discover that all that glitters is not gold. There have been many songs that reflect misinterpreted feelings or appearances and usually to the surprise of someone who thought they had insider's knowledge of the person, situation, or experience. *Rusting Toys* is a book that attempts to bring to the forefront the need for people to ask questions or to report anything that they suspect to be something other than "gold." It is an attempt to get the reader to discover the importance of relying on God and His Son, Jesus Christ.

Enjoy the book.

CHAPTER ONE

Meet the Parents and Grandparents

Before I share the stories of each of my siblings, I feel it is important to build for you an understanding of where my father and mother came from. Insight into their family history will allow you to draw the parallels between how they were raised and what was repeated from their pasts when they had us children. You'll see the destructive cycles more clearly. All of this is told from my memory and through stories I heard passed down and I share them to the best of my recollection. My hope is that you will see that these cycles need to be broken and to raise awareness of destructive patterns either in your family history or in those around you so that no child will have to live under the dark shadows of abuse.

The Douglas Side

My grandparents on my father's side were John and Maude Douglas of Mississippi. John, or "Papa" as he was usually called, was Scotch/Irish. Maude, or "Maudie" as she was sometimes called, was of English descent. Although she had the looks of an Englishwoman, my dad said she had some Cherokee Indian blood in her. I guess that is something that will remain forever unconfirmed.

Papa was a farmer. As I said, he was originally from Mississippi, but he moved to Louisiana some time before my father was born. I knew my grandparents only after they had retired, but rumor has it that he was not a very good businessman. My mom said he allowed people to take advantage of him and take from him without putting up any fight. My dad worked on Papa's rather large farm, but I will provide more on that further along. Maudie was an ordinary housewife. Every time I was ever in their home, it was immaculately clean and smelled wonderful. By the time I knew of them, they lived in West Monroe, Louisiana in a small, white, wood-frame house. The bathroom was "a little shack out back" at first, with indoor facilities that came along eventually. There was no farm.

I have no idea what kind of money Papa made from farming, but it could not have been that much because the family was in deep poverty as they raised their children.

Papa was quiet and soft-spoken. He spoke slowly and muzzled, having to stop and think at frequent intervals to get to what it was he was trying to tell you. He was a thin man and I never saw him in anything but pajamas except for his and Maudie's fiftieth wedding anniversary. My only memories of him were when he had become old and very ill. If he wasn't in his rocking chair, he was in bed. His eyes were piercing blue—so blue that they were almost clear. I heard that at one time he had a very hot temper, but I never saw it. My mom told me that he was very angry at her when I was born because I was born just after midnight on January 16th instead of coming on January 15th, his birthday. Even in his weak condition, Papa always managed to give a hug and a smile when his grandchildren paid him a visit.

Maudie was a loud and busy woman. I'd say she was borderline hyperactive and it was almost impossible to get a word in edgewise when she was speaking. She was short, stout, and moved quickly on her feet. I dreaded her great big bear hugs because she would kiss the face repeatedly and breathe heavily in the ear. Maudie dressed well and almost always wore jewelry. My brothers, sisters, and I were guaranteed a peanut butter sandwich when we visited. My dad made us tell her that we wanted one whenever she asked. Little did anyone know that I hated peanut butter sandwiches when I was a child. She always smelled good, though, and any time I asked her for anything, she gave it to me. Her house was full of curios. One time, I was staring up at a little red ceramic cardinal she had on a shelf and she asked me what I was looking at. When I told her, she asked if I would like it. I said, "Yes!" My parents didn't want me to have it, but she insisted. That cardinal still exists today. She also made a quilt and had my dad take it home to me.

Papa and Maudie were Southern Baptist by denomination and stern believers in attending church. Their Bibles were always in plain sight. They made their children go to Sunday school every Sunday and this was one of my dad's fondest memories. There was a story going around for some time that Papa was a lay preacher but my dad said that it wasn't true. As soft-spoken as he was, it would be hard to imagine it because, back then, if a preacher wasn't making fire and brimstone fall from the sky, he wasn't preaching.

Papa and Maudie brought ten children into the world. One, Cary, died as a child so they raised nine children in a strict and structured home. Papa was a disciplinarian and, I am told, so was Maudie. His beatings were sometimes brutal and his children held just as much fear of him as they did respect. There were not enough bedrooms for each child to have his own room or even his own bed. Everyone worked on the farm. The girls helped the boys out in the field, but they also helped their mother cook and clean in the house. She taught them to cook, clean, and sew. Back then, women got together with their neighbors to make quilts. The girls had a lot of work. They used every scrap of material they could get their hands on to make the quilts. The scraps came from what was left after the dresses were made. Oh yes, almost all of the clothing that the females wore were homemade. They canned the vegetables and fruit that was taken from the field. That, too, was a community project with many neighbors and relatives joining in to get it done.

In addition to the field work, the boys also fed the chickens, cows, mule, and pigs as well as mended fences, repaired barns, built hen houses, and repaired the house. Remember, this was a family in poverty, so the shoes the guys wore were either too small, too big, worn out, hand-me-downs, or non-existent. Can you imagine a thirteen or fourteen year old boy plowing *barefoot* behind a mule in a field full of hard dirt clods? It wasn't uncommon. My dad's feet were in terrible shape by the time he left this world. When they finally did get a tractor, the boys worked on that, too. They were also the ones who drew water from the well for cooking or taking baths and the ones who cut firewood. Their house was heated by a wood stove.

As hard as they all worked together, that's how they played together as well. Their best friends were their brothers and sisters so there was always camaraderie in fun. This family loved to laugh. Most of them had great sense of humors; especially my dad. They shared stories of the shenanigans that they pulled on one another and on Papa. If there is one thing that they never forgot as they aged, it was the stories of having fun and laughing together. Although the neighbors were separated by acres and acres of land, I am quite sure that the laughter from nine children was pretty easy to hear.

Uncle Marshall was the oldest son and he married a lady named Fannie. Uncle Marshall had a laugh that could be heard miles down the road. He didn't really have a career when he and Aunt Fannie got married, so they and their four children lived in an old school bus and worked as sharecroppers. One time he brought the check home to Aunt Fannie—a very sweet, reasonable, and talented lady—and it was less than $500 for a year of hard work! She looked at it, then she looked up at him and said, "Get bathed and dressed. We're going to town to look for jobs."

They moved into a house and Uncle Marshall fixed up the school bus. He asked the school board if he could work for them, picking up children and taking them to school. They said yes, and paid him a little for it. He eventually became a carpenter and did pretty well—well enough to buy a nice home in West Monroe, Louisiana. One year, someone gave him and Aunt Fannie a brand new white Lincoln for an anniversary gift. From then on, he began buying and refurbishing old Fords, Lincolns, and Mercurys for himself. Next to my Uncle Webb and Aunt Clotile, they were my favorite. Uncle Marshall lived well into his nineties.

Uncle Jim married a very pretty lady named Annie Sue. He moved to Mississippi in 1946 and became a welder. He did that for his entire career. Uncle Jim had a strong Christian faith and was a deacon in his church. He and Aunt Annie Sue raised two daughters. My dad and Uncle Jim looked a lot alike and were about the same height and build. He passed away at age 83.

My dad, Hosea E. Douglas, Sr. was the third oldest son. I am going to pass over him for now and skip to Uncle Jack. Uncle Jack joined the Navy in World War II at about the same time that my dad joined the Army Air-Force. He married a very sweet lady named Edna Ruth and they raised two boys and a girl in West Monroe, Louisiana. Uncle Jack ran cabinet and flooring companies for other people. He was well thought of and received a large ranch-style home from a customer. He had a quick-wit and loved to laugh. Uncle Jack raised pigs as well as a lot of the food that his family ate. He passed away in his early to mid-fifties.

Uncle Bill was the baby brother. Despite his intelligence, he flunked out at Louisiana State University and went to work at International Paper in Bastrop, Louisiana. He married a lady named Hazel and they lived in the small town of Swartz, Louisiana. He built his own home and there they raised two boys and one girl. Later in life, Uncle Bill would go from house to house belonging to his siblings just to see if everyone was O.K. He passed away in 2014 in his eighties.

The oldest daughter was my Aunt Clotile. She was a riot! Aunt Clotile was my favorite blood aunt. No one could ever accuse her of not speaking her mind. Papa loved all of his children, but he loved this one a little differently than he should have. She was afraid of what he might do if they were alone. She married a man named Webb Wink and I believe they had five children. I spent more time at their house than I did any of my relatives because they were fun to be around. My cousins were more like my brothers and sisters. Aunt Clotile was a housewife and a great cook as were all her sisters. She passed away in her mid-nineties.

Aunt Maude lived in Pineville, Louisiana. She married a man named Dwight. I don't know if she ever worked, but the years I knew her she was a housewife and great cook. They had four children. She went to the Beauty Shop every week up until she got sick and passed away in 2013.

My Aunt Navy Gay was unbelievably sweet and a great cook as well. She married a man named Dick Hendrix and they had a home in Monroe, Louisiana for years until they moved to Pollock, Louisiana. She was a housewife and I used to stop at her house in Pollock on my way back from Monroe when I lived in Pineville, Louisiana. Every single time I did she insisted on cooking for me. They raised a daughter and a son. She passed away when she was in her eighties.

Aunt Etta Mae (Jinx) lived in West Monroe, Louisiana

with her husband Ed. She was the baby daughter. They had one child; a son who I consider a friend. Aunt Etta Mae loved to laugh and loved to have company at her house. She worked two and three jobs because she had to. Uncle Ed had a small heart attack long before he was forty and claimed he couldn't work anymore, leaving Aunt Etta Mae to earn the money. I would help her with the yard work because, apparently, Uncle Ed couldn't do yard work either. However, he didn't have a problem going over to the Masons unit he belonged to and cooking all day for them. They lived in Maudie's house after she passed away. Aunt Etta Mae once told me that she thought she would have to work until she dropped and that is exactly what happened. She passed away in her early eighties.

Now, I'll tell you about my dad, Hosea E. Douglas, Sr. Dad was the child that Papa took out of school every time the fence needed mending or the barn needed a new roof. Dad worked in bare feet and did not own a pair of shoes until he was sixteen years of age. Because of this, he dropped out of school while in the seventh grade; a grade he repeated several times. He joined the Army Air-Force during World War II and was stationed in North Africa with the most decorated bombardment group of the war. While in the military, he met my mom and they married after he got home from North Africa. They settled in Monroe, Louisiana and he built his own house, buying wood and other materials as they were able to afford it. The house only had three bedrooms and four beds. There was a lot of sharing bed space. They bought the property from a lady named Lucille Ball. You know I can't make something like that up. She lived down the street.

For many years, my dad couldn't hold down a job. Every time a boss would say or do something he didn't like, he would walk out. They were so poor that, at times, they would go to the neighbors and beg for something to eat.

Despite their poverty, they kept having children. Finally, Uncle Jack told him about the pulp and paper plant he was helping to build in West Monroe, Louisiana and that they were hiring for all positions. Dad went for an interview. When he got home he informed Mom that they offered him a job right on the spot, but he didn't think he was going to take it. Mom called Uncle Jack and begged him to call Dad and convince him to take the job. It is sad that Dad needed convincing that he needed a job, but he did. By this time he had six children and no car. He and Uncle Jack had owned a gasoline station at one time that led to bankruptcy. They lost everything except the house.

The children kept coming. Most of our relatives on both sides had indoor plumbing, but Dad and Mom didn't. Dad, Mom, and whatever children were able to work planted crops on our 3.2 acres and raised pigs and chickens. My dad's relatives pitched in when it came time to bring in the crops and helped out with canning.

Dad was a handsome man. All of his brothers and brothers-in-law wanted to hang out with him because he was outgoing and humorous. People liked him and found him to be personable. He would bring home his paycheck faithfully most of the time, but every now and then something within him drove him to go out and get drunk. He was also a womanizer. When Mom smelled the liquor on him, she would remind him that he had little mouths to feed and should be spending his money on them instead of alcohol. I think the pressure of having so many kids and so little money took a toll on him because over time he began to lose his temper when Mom would suggest he stop drinking. He started beating on her. His anger escalated and soon, he was beating all of us children for seemingly no reason. He used a belt, tree limbs, his belt buckle, and eventually began to use a hard rubber strap he got from work.

Dad left bruises and whelps on all of us. Mom's eyes were often blackened. Dad hit her in the head so much, I'm surprised he didn't cause brain damage or kill her. Once, when Mom was expecting, Dad lost his temper, kicked her in the stomach, and she lost the baby boy she carried. Sometimes when he got home he would line us up against a wall in the dining room and beat each one of us, making us confess to doing something wrong while he was at work—whether we did or not. This led to all of us picking up the habit of lying. The mental and emotional abuse made us very much afraid of him and confused about what love was because he would beat us and yell at us all year long, but then at Christmas, he showered us with gifts. He would hug us and treat us kindly on that day, and the rest of the year we lived in fear.

He was a funny man, though. He had a dry sense of humor and a quick wit. Dad would keep a straight face, not looking at anyone, and say something so funny that everyone in the room would be laughing except for him. He shared stories of growing up, going to school, and World War II.

My dad was a talented man and a workaholic. Uncle Jack used to say that all of my dad's brothers wanted to be able to use their hands like he could. Carpentry, plumbing, running electric wiring, working on cars—it all came easy to him. After working eight hours at his job, he would come home, drink a cup of coffee, drink a glass of water, and take all of us children and our mom out to the field to work on the crops until it was dark. We always had dinner late.

After having us eight kids, Dad went back to school and finished his education completely. He was then promoted to the engineering department at Manville. Dad was raised Southern Baptist, but he never went to church after he married my mom. She was Roman Catholic. After Dad got his education he converted to Catholicism. After his promotion, the frequency of beatings reduced greatly. He began showing more love to all of his children, but he was a little bit too attentive to his daughters. Does that sound familiar?

Once the money started coming in, we got a new car about every other year. We really didn't need them, but he insisted on getting them. When you do without for so long, sometimes you go overboard. We had new furniture too and finally there were enough beds for everyone to have their own. The money changed everything. We got more and better clothing and ate like kings. Dad quit raising food because he didn't need to anymore. He stopped beating Mom, too. I contribute that to going to church as well as having more than enough money. However, he was still a workaholic.

Instead of coming home and working in the field, he would make all five of his sons help him as he either added on or improved the house, worked on a car (his or Mom's), or with any other project he had taken up. It never stopped. He woke us up early on Saturday mornings to put us to work doing something. Occasionally he'd take the whole family fishing or crawfishing on Saturday or Sunday. He bought outside toys and games for us, too. We got baseball gear, croquet, badminton, tennis, tether ball, football, and other equipment. Once, he brought home 55 gallon ink barrels for us to barrel-walk on. All of us children played together and we laughed more and more. Still, on occasion, he would abuse us physically, mentally, or emotionally. The confusion of that always lingered like a fog.

The older he got, the more loving and caring he became. He didn't get drunk like he used to. I watched a long process of mellowing on his part. He began boasting about his children instead of looking for faults as he had when we lived under his roof. Dad began telling his children that he loved us on the phone or when we were about to leave from a visit and he always had to hug on our arrival and at our departure.

He and Mom sold the house he built and moved into the Monroe city limits into a very nice home. It was much smaller than the one he had built, but, again, he had added onto the old house making it twice as large as it was when he first built it. Even after all of his sons had been out of his house for a number of years, when we went to visit, he still made us go out and help him work on the house or in his yard. My brothers and I said that we were indentured servants for life. Not too many years after he bought the new house, he retired. He was sixty-two years of age. He really didn't want to retire, but he had seen so many of the men who started at Manville get fired for no reason as they got older just so Manville wouldn't have to pay retirement. Dad wasn't stupid and he wasn't taking any chances. He built furniture, planted flowers in his yard, and for a couple of years leased a small strip of land along with my brother Larry in order to raise a vegetable garden.

He and my mom loved their grandchildren and showered them with the love that they had never shown us as children. They spoiled them by providing them with expensive gifts and taking some of them on expensive vacations all over the United States. Dad and Mom baby-sat while the parents were at work. They had their favorites, but my dad loved one of his granddaughters a little more than he should have. . .and so the cycle repeats.

In the mid-80s, Dad began to say that he thanked God that my mom stayed with him all those years and that his children still came to see him in spite of what he had done. My dad was in excellent health until the last year of his life. One day in February of 2003, my dad was outside and my mom was near the kitchen window when, according to my mom, a voice not of this world called my dad by name. When Dad came into the house, my mom told him what she heard and asked if he heard it. Dad didn't answer, but walked away from her with his head down. He'd heard it. He was in and out of the hospital from February of 2003 until June of the same year. They found that he had hernias and repaired them, but he became infected by metal poisoning. His white blood count ran into the thousands and his eyes were set in the back of his head. I spent every night of his last ten days on earth with him in the hospital. With one or two nights of exception, it was just me and Dad after hours. When they said his death was imminent, I went back to Dallas to get some things done, planning to return later that day. However, my mom phoned me and told me that he had passed away.

Congressman Ralph Hall of Rockwall, Texas (a good friend of mine) had just presented him with a flag that had been flown over the capital of the U. S. in honor of his service to his country. Three fighter jets flew over at his funeral service to salute him. This was fitting as his time in the military was his most treasured time. Dad was eighty-five years of age when he passed away in June of 2003.

The Soileau Side

My grandparents on my mom's side were Onezime (Pop-Pop) Soileau and Alexandrine (Mom-Mom) Vidrine Soileau. They were Cajun French and brought up in South Louisiana. They settled in Opelousas, Louisiana.

Pop-Pop worked for the railroad almost all of his life. He made very good money, but somehow they were always poor. Even after he retired from the railroad, he still wore khaki clothing all the time. Mom-Mom was a housewife and not a very good one at that. Their house was always dark with the shades pulled down. What made it even darker was the black furniture. The house was always in a mess and had an unidentifiable odor that lurked within. They had an outhouse at one time, but by the time I started school, there was indoor plumbing in their house. They had it much sooner than my parents did.

Pop-Pop had a quick temper and I watched him lose it many, many times. He would cuss and swear in French. He was a strict disciplinarian with his daughters, but not too much with his son. I don't think Pop-Pop liked little children much. Every time our family would go to visit, he would go out on his front porch with his chewing tobacco and the pint of whiskey he kept in his right hip pocket. He sipped on whiskey all day long.

Mom-Mom was distant. Every now and then she would talk to me, but it wasn't much. I can remember her laughing and grabbing me to dance with her only once to the sound of the radio that they always had playing in their house. Her clothes were drab. She wasn't a very good cook. Nearly every time we visited we ate red beans and rice and sausage... maybe. I don't have an official diagnosis, but signs showed that Mom-Mom was mentally ill. She mentally and emotionally abused her children. I was afraid to walk in their house because it felt like something evil was inside. If I had not had my parents and brothers and sisters with me, I would not have been able to walk into that house.

Pop-Pop and Mom-Mom were Roman Catholic and lived very close to St. Landry's Cathedral. The priest there was good buddies with Pop-Pop. Pop-Pop and Mom-Mom drilled it into their children's heads that only Catholics could go to heaven. They made sure that their children went to Mass every Sunday and they sent them to a Catholic School. The family was too poor to be able to afford the cost of the school, but since Pop-Pop and the pastor were such good buddies, they got to go for free. There, it was drilled even deeper into the children's heads that if you were not Catholic, you were going to hell. I guess you can call what they did "brainwashing."

My grandparents raised three children in that house in Opelousas. They had one son and two daughters. The children were expected to help around the house, but they didn't have to work nearly as hard as the children on my father's side did. Pop-Pop and Mom-Mom always had a garden up until the time Pop-Pop felt he was too old to take care of it. It was hard to figure out Pop-Pop and Mom-Mom's relationship. We saw two sides to them, sometimes in the same minute. Mom-Mom would be busy cooking in the kitchen and Pop-Pop would hug her and love on her one minute and the next thing I knew they were yelling and cussing at one another. When Mom-Mom died at age seventy-two, Pop-Pop was lost.

The night before she passed away, my parents, my brother Larry, and I heard the back door of our house open. We checked it, but it was locked tight. After everyone went back to bed, I saw a cloud-like figure floating near the ceiling in my room. It made its way down beside me and a voice like Mom-Mom's, but not of this world, whispered in my ear. I couldn't make out what it said and I was very afraid. I squeezed my eyes tight and went back to sleep. At the funeral home, Pop-Pop stayed right beside her coffin ninety-nine percent of the time. He was very loving that day. He picked up each of us children so that we could see her and give her a kiss. Pop-Pop mourned her passing so much that he passed away one year after she did at age seventy-five. Everyone cried at her funeral except me. I felt the evil was gone.

Isaac was the oldest and was the apple of his father's eye. According to my mom and her sister, he was never disciplined like they were. If he did anything wrong, one of the girls got punished for it (and it was usually my mom). Uncle Isaac was a really smart man, but he was a thief. He worked at an auto parts store. He stole from his parents and from my mom and her sister. When we went to Pop-Pop's funeral, we had a new car and he broke into it to steal money. He knew my mom always went to visit with as much money as she could and that she stored and locked it in the car. After Pop-Pop was buried, we went back to the car and found it broken into. The first word out of my mom's mouth was, "Isaac!" He came to the car and admitted that he had *borrowed* some money from them. Of course, he never bothered paying it back. He married a very sweet woman named Ella and they had two daughters and a son. Uncle Isaac had been married once before and had children, but he wasn't in their lives. He beat on Ella and was very strict with his children. He made them give him money after they started to work and this provided him with a beautiful home. I guess he felt they owed him for putting them through college. Uncle Isaac passed away in Chalmette, Louisiana at age seventy-seven. He had money when he died.

My aunt Dee was the baby. She was a nurse by profession and she moved around a lot. Aunt Dee was always unhappy. She lived with Pop-Pop and Mom-Mom until shortly after they passed away. I know she had lived in Opelousas, Lafayette, Baton Rouge, and maybe other places. She had been married once and had a son named Andrew. The marriage didn't last long, but her son kept in touch with his father until his death. She talked bad about everybody and was a miserable woman. She and my mom could not get along, but they couldn't stay away from one another very long. Her son never married and always lived with her. Most of his life, he slept in the same bed with her; even in adulthood. Aunt Dee was a terrible cook. When we went to visit, it was always red beans and rice and sausage... maybe. Does that sound familiar?

After my dad passed away, Aunt Dee would play on my mom's sympathies to get money from her. She would call and say that she and her son were starving so Mom would go down and give her money. However, Mom noticed that every time she went to visit, Aunt Dee had new things in her house. She passed away in her eighties.

And then there was my mom, Mary Soileau Douglas. Like Aunt Dee, my mom was also a nurse. She had been a housewife until my baby brother started school. She and my sister Pat went to nursing school together in order for my mom to help Pat in school. However, my mom started her nursing career a year before Pat did. She worked at St. Francis Medical Center in Monroe for a year or two then switched to a nursing home where she stayed until she retired. She had been the head nurse on the eleven to seven shifts. Mom had been a nurse when she was younger, but had given it up when she married my father. She was very smart in school. About the time she began nursing again, Dad had finished his education and was making a lot more money. With both of them making good salaries, people began to say that we were rich. I must admit that we were living comfortably, but I never considered us wealthy. Money didn't change Mom much on the inside, other than she was able to have nicer things and buying the things she wanted was not a problem anymore.

Mom was a little shy and introverted. All the way up until a couple of years before my dad passed away, Mom was unsure of herself. Mom had been emotionally and mentally abused by her own mother. Mom-Mom used to take her and her little sister to the well to draw water. She'd put Aunt Dee in the bucket and let her down in the well. Mom-Mom would laugh at my mom because she was so frightened and would cry and scream; begging her mother to stop. Mom-Mom and Pop-Pop would pick up the other two children, set them in their laps, love and kiss on them, then laugh and point to my mom sitting on the floor looking up and say, "Look at ole jealous!"

She cried herself to sleep. Mom was very unhappy for most of her life. As sick as this may sound, she used to tell my dad to beat us as soon as he got in from work while she sat in her favorite chair observing. She took it all in and looked as if she enjoyed it. I guess maybe she was glad because if Dad was beating on us, it meant he wasn't beating on her. Of course Dad did beat on her and cheated on her as well. She always pointed out our faults and could never forgive anyone. If she was angry at one of us, she expected all of her other children to be angry, too. Some did just what she said. She held grudges forever. If someone did something to her when they were six years old, she held it against them still at age sixty and never forgave or forgot.

She was generous though with money once we had it. Mom gave her children money and bought almost anything that they asked for. She believed in helping her children and anyone else in need. People took advantage of her; especially some of her children and one of her grandchildren. Her sister, and later her sister's son, tried to bleed her dry.

Mom was a beautiful woman when she was young. In fact, she was so beautiful that one time, a photographer had to figure out how to take her portrait to do her beauty justice. He put a camera behind her without her knowing it, had her pose for the camera in front, and told her he had to leave the room but he would be right back. When he re-entered the room, she turned her head to look behind her and he took the photo.

My mom was a die-hard Catholic. She believed that if you were not Catholic, you were going to hell. Mom used to tell us that the Catholic Church was the "one true church instituted by Christ and unless you belong, you are going to hell." She drilled Catholicism into us and made us go to church every Sunday and any holy days of obligation. If it is possible for someone's religion to send them to hell, then there are many people like my mom burning right now. However, my mom said she loved her Jesus. She prayed constantly. My dad converted to Catholicism by listening to her help her children with catechism lessons.

Mom had a temper. She abused us physically, mentally, and emotionally. Mom loved to slap her children in the face. My mom faked taking an overdose and faked having a loaded pistol to shoot herself with in order to scare all of us. Once, when she was upset with my sister Helen, she told us that if Helen called the house to tell Helen that Mom had died in an automobile accident. After one time when Dad had been beating on her, she loaded up his shotgun and went after him. In 1976, she told me and only me that she had gone to see an attorney to divorce my dad. The attorney talked her out of it. She did not want her sons to get married. Mom was jealous of our girlfriends and wives.

Mom was never a very good cook. However, she made the best homemade biscuits and the best beef roast that I ever tasted. She was really comical about her cooking. Every time one of her sons introduced her to a fiancé, the first question she would ask is "do you cook?" Then she would proceed to tell them that she was not a very good cook and she could not understand how all of her children were. She would say that her sons were better cooks than her daughters.

As Mom got older, she became more tolerant and not as much of an introvert. She loved to have her children and grandchildren visit and would cook breakfast all the way until the time of her death. She kept her house clean too. I must say that her temper never subsided though. Mom could pitch a fit better than anyone I ever knew. My dad used to say she was "kicking out of her traces." She got funnier as she aged. Mom used laugh and tell Dad that she was smarter than him. He would reply, "I'll tell you one thing. You're a fast learner." Mom went through a lot of positive changes before she passed away at age ninety-four (very close to ninety-five). She no longer felt that only Catholics could go to heaven and she even listened to protestant preachers on television. She liked some of them a lot.

CHAPTER TWO

Patricia
"Pat"

After my dad married my mom, they went to her parents' house to get her things. As dad stepped back on the front porch after loading the car, he noticed a little girl standing next to my mom.

"Whose is that?" he asked.

"Mine. Do you mind?" Mom replied.

And that is how Dad said he learned of my half-sister, Patricia. She was the oldest of my siblings. My dad had been in the military, stationed overseas. He knew my mom had someone in her life previously, which he assumed was a boyfriend, but Mom said she had been married to a man who was Pat's father and that man died.

I have my own suspicions.

We never knew the name of this mysterious dead first husband of my mother's, nor were there any papers that ever documented such. My mom made a point to tell me often that Pop-Pop was very respectful toward her and her sister when they grew into women. I believe she told me that so often because she was trying to convince herself that was the case. I am going to say something here that many people will not like. Pat and my cousin Andrew (Aunt Dee's son) looked a lot alike. So much so, it was almost as if they had the same father. They were close to one another too; almost like brother and sister. The non-accounting of Pat's father's identity, combined with the fact that Aunt Dee's husband left quite soon after Andrew was born, leads me to wonder how respectful Pop-Pop was.

At any rate, Pat was sick as an infant and toddler. She almost died. Mom prayed for her every day and dedicated her to the Virgin Mary. Mom dressed her in Mary's colors of blue and white until she was finally "out of the woods." That was the promise she had made to the Virgin Mary in her prayers. Pat had learning difficulties and so did Andrew. Pat liked to read and to learn, but she had a tough time with it. She learned to walk and talk much later than what is typical.

Because Dad and Mom were so poor, she didn't have many toys and the ones she had were often homemade. I am told that she played well with others even though she was shy. When it was time for her to start the first grade, my parents enrolled her in a Catholic school. I am certain that they could not afford to send her, so somehow she must have received a scholarship for poor children. Pat struggled throughout her school years. However, she made friends easily, which helped her come out of her shyness.

By the time Pat was in high school, she was well-liked and developed a laugh that was contagious. She still had trouble learning and repeated a couple of grades. This bothered her well into adulthood. She did graduate from high school and already knew that she wanted to become a nurse.

While in nursing school, she began working at St. Francis Medical Center as a nurse's aide. My mom enrolled with her in order to help Pat get through school. She struggled and used to cry about her test grades. Once the course was completed, she and Mom drove to New Orleans to take the state board exam. Pat failed it, and Mom passed it. Mom said that she thought the board got the grades mixed up because she didn't know the answers to many of the questions. I don't know if that is true, but I'm pretty sure she was trying to make Pat feel better. It was during this time that it was revealed that Pat was not Dad's child. Pat cried her eyes out about it. Pat had every reason to resent the fact that Dad wasn't her dad.

Dad beat her and abused her physically the longest because she was the oldest. Pat was ten years older than me. When I was in the fourth grade, she was a senior in high school. When we got indoor plumbing, Dad used a door on the bathroom that he had removed from another room some time before. There was a tiny hole in the middle of it and through it, he tried to watch Pat bathe. The hole was too small, so he took his knife and enlarged it big enough to peep through. Pat realized what was going on and went to my mom in tears. Mom was the angriest I had ever seen her. She called him all kinds of names. The next day, I heard my mom and Pat discussing how to cover the hole. I had been putting a model car together and it came with a small tube of a bondo-like material. I took that material and put it on the hole. Once hardened, it was indestructible. Dad tried to look though it the next morning and learned he had been foiled.

Pat had other reasons to resent him, too. Her whole life to that point, she lived in neglect. She received very little food and what food she got wasn't at all proper. Her clothes were mere rags that had been handed down from cousins, and kids at school made fun of her. One of the neighbor's daughters (Anna) told everyone at school that Pat and the rest of us took off our good rags when we got home from school and put on worse rags. This was true. Before the indoor bath was built, we all took baths in a number ten galvanized tub. This was especially hard for the girls because Mom and the other girls had to hold up sheets around them so my dad and the neighbors couldn't see.

Pat had been beaten with a belt, a tree limb, a belt buckle, and a hard rubber strap. She had felt Dad's hand both opened and closed in a fist. She had been yelled at in public and called unflattering names by this man she thought was her father. If we were out of milk for breakfast before school, she and my sister Helen were sent out on foot (even in freezing weather) to a store a long way from the house. She had been made to cook and prepare Dad's lunch when Mom wasn't able. Pat had not been shown the love that every child should be shown by her parents. She was Mom's favorite, but that didn't save her.

My sister was always afraid. It didn't matter what it was, she was afraid of it. She lived in constant fear. Pat was afraid of heights, afraid of being locked in a room (even if it was a very large room), afraid of being in water, afraid of being turned upside down, afraid to cross the street, afraid of the dark, afraid to fall from a bicycle, afraid to take a test, afraid to try new things, afraid to ride in a fast-moving car, and just afraid of life in general.

If it had not been for my oldest brother Hosea (Bubba) encouraging her when she went to nursing school the second time, I don't believe she would have had the confidence to work hard and pass her state board exam. I went with my mom and Pat to New Orleans the day that she took the exam the second time. She finished it quickly and she was confident. She passed.

Pat got a job as a nurse at St. Francis Medical Center and began to buy her own clothes. She had excellent taste. Most of her money went into a savings account at the bank. Pat knew how to save and budget. Turns out, she was very good at it. That job really gave her confidence. The patients loved her. Very often patients would give her gifts when it was time for them to go home. Some of them stayed in touch with Pat long after their stay. She was a hard worker and genuinely cared about people.

Pat began to give Mom money to help out with the

grocery bill. We ate so much better then. She even helped buy us school clothes. At Christmas, we could all count on Pat to get us what we wanted. If we didn't let it be known what we wanted, we would still get a very nice gift. She loved her brothers and sisters. When I began to rebel in high school, it was Pat who encouraged me and never turned her back on me as some of the others did. When we were all married and/or moved away, Pat would be so glad to see us.

She didn't date much in high school, but that changed when she began working as a nurse. Not only were men attracted to her outside beauty, but her inside beauty and that newfound confidence as well. It didn't hurt that she loved to laugh and had that contagious laugh I mentioned earlier. A couple of men wanted to marry her, but things didn't work out for one reason or another. She used to tell us what her dream husband would be and look like, but then she would say, "You watch. I'll probably marry some fat guy." She was correct. She did. He was very nice to her when they dated and when they first got married.

Pat had Christian values. She would never let a man touch her in a disrespectful way. I say that because Pat got pregnant very soon after she was married and almost lost her life giving birth to her son. He ended up being her only child because of the damage she sustained bringing him into this world. Pat was a devout Roman Catholic and insisted that her husband be the same. They raised their son likewise. She had many prayer books and read them daily. Pat and Frank seemed to have a good marriage, but Pat's countenance changed along the course of her married years. Mom said Pat had to wait on him hand and foot like a slave. He bought her a home, but never did one thing to maintain it. I went over to her house every week for a while so that I could mow her lawn for her. He was too lazy to do it. He had no pride. She was embarrassed for people to see the inside of her house and eventually would not allow anyone inside. She sacrificed a lot for her husband and son.

Pat began gaining weight right after she got married and continued to do so. She reached a very unhealthy weight and her health deteriorated as she aged. Sadly, Pat became very selfish. She was like a different person from the generous older sister I grew up with. My wife and child and I lived in a house behind hers in Alexandria, Louisiana for a short time. I used to walk or drive to her house to visit with her pretty often. Then, one very cold winter, my car broke down and, being a student, I didn't have the money to repair it. This meant that neither I nor my wife could go to work and our baby could not go to daycare. I called Pat and asked for a loan that I would repay the very next Friday. She hung up on me. The next day, we bundled up the baby and began walking to the baby-sitter's house (Pat's neighbor) in the freezing cold. She, her husband, and her child passed us by in her car and she looked away. Pat called my sister Helen later that day and talked badly about me for asking to loan fifty dollars until Friday. I wasn't angry that Pat wouldn't borrow me the money, I was angry that she allowed our baby to have to walk in the freezing cold. She remained selfish the rest of her life.

When Dad passed away, Mom had my baby sister living with her. Mom told her that they were going to clean up the yard and sell the house. The neighborhood had changed and not for the better. It became dangerous to live there. Selfish Pat asked Mom, "Well, if you move away, what am I supposed to do?" As a result, Mom didn't move. Pat was still her mom's baby and anything that Pat wanted from her, she got.

Every time Pat found out that one of her brothers or sisters wanted something that belonged to Mom or Dad, she would run ahead of them, ask Mom for it, and she got it. One day Dad was saying that some of his children couldn't wait for him to "kick the bucket" so that they could get everything he had. I laughed. He asked me why I was laughing. I told him the only thing that I wanted of his was his shaving mug. I explained that I had watched him shave with it from the time I was two and it meant something to me. He said that I shouldn't want the thing because it had been broken and glued back together a hundred times. Still, I persisted and he said I could have it. As soon as he passed away, Pat went to Mom's house and snatched it. I do have it now because when Pat passed away, Mom gave it to me. That's just one example of the greed that grew in her heart. Where that seed of selfishness came from, I'll never know.

By the time she passed away, Pat didn't have many friends. Her best friend had always been my sister Helen. In general, Pat had good relationships with all of her brothers and sisters. There were times when she would be on the outs with one of us, but she always managed to get us back. She and Helen resolved their last falling out before she passed away. Most of her disagreements were brought on either by her selfishness or trying to appease Mom when she was angry at someone. Pat did not die happy. She was going to several physicians for various reasons. Pat had to clean her system out for some tests that a doctor was doing on Monday. Sunday night she asked Frank to take her to the hospital because something wasn't right. She was afraid of the tests. Lazy Frank told her that he would drop her off, but he wasn't staying. He said she could call him when she was ready to go back home. She never did. She passed away in her sleep that night at age sixty-two.

CHAPTER THREE

Helen

Helen was my dad's first child and his favorite daughter. He must have been very proud of her because she is the only one of his children that he took to a portrait studio to have her toddler portrait made.

As an infant and a toddler, Helen endured the pains of hunger and the lack of shelter and proper clothing. The house that Dad had built was extremely drafty. In fact, the outside doors at the back and on the side of the house banged through the night when the wind blew. Helen and Pat were often sick with colds and the flu.

As a child, I climbed up in the attic of my parents' house and found two red wooden things that I could not identify. I pulled one down and Helen told me it was a doll stroller that Dad made for her and Pat when they were children. It was shaped somewhat like a wheel barrow, but much smaller, and it had one long handle to push with. It had two wooden wheels that rolled pretty well. They would put the dolls in the bucket portion or wheel barrow portion. Helen laughed as she told the stories of playing with them.

Helen was outgoing, even as a child. All the kids liked her, and she was a favorite of many of her teachers. I'm sure it helped that she was smart in school. Helen understood everything she was taught and was very talented. Dad taught her how to write and to this day her handwriting is practically identical to his. Dad was talented in drawing and he passed that on to Helen, too. I think the boys thought Helen was pretty, but from first grade through high school she never really had a steady boyfriend. Helen had a lot of girlfriends in high school. Her friends would pick her up on weekends and during the summer so they could go to the movies, the drive-in restaurant, or do other fun things. They would go bicycle riding for hours at a time.

Although she began going to the Catholic school, at some point she and the other children began going to the public school. Like I said, she was smart. As soon as she got home from school, she would sit down right away and begin her homework. I guess she was one of the few of us who didn't need much help with her school work. As I recall, other girls would come over or call to get her help with their school work. Helen was the first of the children to graduate with honors and her graduating class was the first to graduate at the new high school in town. My dad and mom were very proud of her.

Helen was very mischievous and loved to laugh. She was always playing jokes and tricking her brothers and sisters. All of us children played together outside, and Helen was always the leader in deciding what we were going to play. When Dad brought home the fifty-five gallon ink barrels from work, it was Helen who decided that we were going to have barrel rolling contests and races. Since the barrels were divided into three parts by seams, she appointed three children to each barrel. It was so much fun. She organized sack races with some burlap sacks we had. I guess my favorite thing that Helen thought of was taking mason jars and catching fireflies at night during the summer. I enjoyed catching them, but it was always a let-down the next day when we found our fireflies dead or not lighting up.

Not only was Helen smart and creative, but she could cook, too. Helen took home economics in high school and was very good at it. When there was money to cook something besides beans, rice, and cornbread, Helen would cook and it was always delicious. Helen could bake delicious cakes. However, Helen being Helen, once she put a secret ingredient in a piece of a chocolate cake that she baked and gave it to my youngest sister, Karen. Karen bit into it and realized that it was not something she should be eating. Mom was furious and told Dad when he got home. He beat Helen for the prank.

After high school, Helen enrolled in the local college. She certainly had the grades and the brains to do well. There was one thing that our parents didn't count on, though. There were a lot more boys at the college than there were at the high school. Boys (young men) were calling the house for her constantly and there were few Friday nights that she didn't have a date. One of our cousins, Marshall, helped her by introducing her around the school. I'm not sure it was really a help. Her grades were good at first, but then she concentrated on the boys more than she did on her classes. She said that she always wanted to be popular and now she was. Why was she so popular? Helen was looking for love, but unfortunately settled for the wrong kind of love and certainly the wrong kind of attention. Not having a good example at home to draw from, she didn't know what the right kind of love looked like. She got a bad reputation. Then she met a young pre-law student named P.A. (Parnell) Stockstill. This was not a good thing.

P.A. drove an old blue Ford Fairlane. He had been in an accident and was suing the other party. I think he figured he could bleed someone for all they were worth, so he walked around with a walking cane wherever he went. He was tall, blonde, and not a very handsome or friendly man. From what Marshall told my parents, P.A. was smart in school. Helen was in love. I'm afraid P.A. wasn't, but he wanted to use

Helen for whatever he could get out of her.

When Helen's grades came to the house, they were not good. She had been cutting her classes to be with P.A. Dad and Mom confronted her with it. There was a big argument and Dad slapped her around like he always liked to do. I can understand his hurt, but the smacking part I will never understand. My parents sent her to a college down in South Louisiana that had a tuition they really couldn't afford, but they wanted to get her away from P.A. Instead of staying there, she called P.A. to come and get her, and he did. When my parents found out about it, they panicked.

Dad and Mom began a frantic search for her, but it did no good. Finally, Dad found P.A. and confronted him with questions as to the whereabouts of Helen. Dad grabbed him by the collar of his shirt and asked him where she was.

P.A. said, "Let go of me old man!"

Dad didn't. He continued to press P.A. and I'm not sure how, but Dad and Mom did find her. Helen ran away from home once afterward and took a bottle of aspirin in an effort to commit suicide.

She worked several jobs, but the first one I remember her working after all that mess was at a motel. I remember this one because Uncle Jack showed up there once with his boss for a meeting. Helen thought she recognized him, but wasn't sure. Uncle Jack signed his boss into the motel and gave the sheet to Helen. She looked down at it and thought that the name on the registration was his. She told him that she thought he looked like her uncle. He asked what her uncle's name was and she told him. He laughed and told her that that was exactly who he was. During the time she worked there, she ran up bills at local clothing stores and Mom had to pay them.

She tried to be an airline stewardess, but she failed the physical. By this time she had colored her hair blonde and was still hanging on to P. A. Stockstill. Still on the outs with my parents, one day, in broad daylight, she and P.A. went to my parents' house, picked up rocks from the driveway, threw them on top of the house, started laughing, then got back in the car and drove away. It hurt my mom deeply. She felt like it was the same as throwing rocks in her face after all she tried to do for Helen.

Somewhere along the way Helen broke up with P.A. and started dating other people. She began to see my parents again. Eventually, she met and married a guy who went to high school with my oldest brother. His name was Pat Welker, and he was the brother of a friend of mine from high school named Bobby Welker. My dad, my sister Pat, and I went to the wedding. The marriage was short-lived. She said that he wouldn't get a job and that his mother was very domineering. She wanted out. She got out.

While working in the office at Montgomery Ward Department Store, she met a local disc jockey named Mitch Craig. He was my oldest brother's age, and was very popular in Monroe. They dated for a long while and eventually got married. Mitch had to go into the Army, so he was not home when their first child was born. However, they had two more children and he was there for both births.

Mitch had better opportunities elsewhere, so they lived in Dallas and then Memphis, where they settled. In Memphis, Mitch became extremely successful. He ran what was probably the largest production company in the U.S., then eventually started his own business. My mom said that he was a millionaire. All I know is that they have money...lots of it.

Ordinarily I would say that this is a good thing, but it has been a very bad thing for Helen. She became selfish and began to feel that her wealth allowed her to do anything she wanted and no one could say a word. Actually, her actions showed that she felt that way all along, but the money made it worse. When Helen's children fall on hard times, they go to her for help, but don't get it. She tells them that she will feed them at her house, but they can't have any money. The year that my dad passed away, everyone went home for Christmas. Most of us bought gifts for each other, but she didn't bother.

When Mitch saw all the gifts he, she, their children, and everyone else were getting, he said to Helen, "I thought you said no one was buying gifts this year?"

She rolled her eyes all around the room and realized that we all knew she was committing just one more act of selfishness. Helen began to meddle in other people's affairs; causing trouble for people and ending relationships. Don't misunderstand me—she wouldn't do this evil on her own, but instead convinced others to do her dirty work.

Her oldest daughter was dating two guys, but preferred one over the other. The lesser liked guy, Lee, telephoned Helen and told her that it looked like he was going to be out of the picture so he was calling to say good-bye. Helen told him to fight for Michelle. He did, and he ended up marrying her. Helen talked to Michelle often on his behalf because she and Mitch found out how much money Lee made. They wanted her to marry for money. According to my sisters and my mom and dad, Helen meddled in their affairs so much that she ended up splitting them up.

She met another guy whose family was filthy rich and Helen pushed her daughter until she married him. Helen also meddled in that until they divorced.

My parents almost went to jail because of her meddling. Helen put a friend of hers up to calling Family Services about my parents' behavior toward the child of a girlfriend of mine. I was at my parents' house when that happened. The mother of the child called me and told me that it was a friend of Helen's (acting on Helen's behalf) who made the call. Years later I confronted Helen about it. She admitted putting the friend up to making the call, but would not admit to telling them that I witnessed the abuse. She has meddled in the affairs of her brothers and sisters as well as her children. As it seems to be a compulsion for her, I don't see how she will never stop.

Meddling in other people's business must be a hard cycle of hatred to break. An example of her continued hostility against others can be seen in what happened just a couple of years ago. Lynn (my wife) and I went to my mom's house for Christmas. While I was in the back taking a shower, Helen sat in the den with my wife and my baby sister. Helen found it necessary to tell my wife hurtful things from my past. Lynn kept it inside for several months before disclosing to me what Helen had said. I e-mailed Helen and told her to stop meddling in my life. There were e-mails exchanged back and forth and of course she felt she had done nothing wrong and I had started something unnecessarily. Often when a person has a problem being an instigator of trouble, he or she will try and get others to fight their fights. Helen does this very thing. If she has a disagreement with one of her brothers or sisters, she gets on the phone and calls all the others, plus her children, nieces, and nephews, to get the troops on her side. She even called my daughter trying to discredit me.

There isn't a single one of us who hasn't had things in our past that we wish had not happened. We all have things we wish we hadn't done. Telling my own daughter and my wife things that happened was not her place, nor should it be anyone's business. I'm blessed to have a wife who says that what I did in the past is in the past. Following that incident, I called government officials in Tennessee and Mississippi. The slander and spreading of information Helen did verbally and through electronic means is illegal and could get her and her daughters jail time for up to ten years. But meddlers don't think of those consequences. They are trying to feed their own sense of worth by putting others down. It is a sad way to live.

Helen tells me that I keep secrets and have kept them all of my life. She would be correct. My mom once said that Helen really knows her Bible. Helen told me that she pays for Bible studies and goes to them during the week. Well, the Bible tells us to keep our private life private. In Ecclesiastes we read that our words should be few:

Do not be hasty in word or impulsive in thought to bring up a matter in the presence of God. For God is in heaven and you are on the earth; therefore let your words be few. For the dream comes through much effort and the voice of a fool through many words (Ecc. 5:2-3).

I learn from this that everything that goes on is not for everyone to hear. Ephesians 4:29-31, 1 Peter 2:1, 1 Timothy 5:13, and James 3:6-8 also give us lessons we should heed. Words can hurt and words can heal. They should be chosen carefully. Helen may not have read those passages.

Helen professes to be a born-again Christian. She converted to the Southern Baptist denomination some years ago. Helen tells me that she has a great relationship with her pastor. Outward demonstrations of selfishness, meddling, gossip, and acts that hurt or cause trouble for others are signs of unhappiness within. The abuse and poverty from which she came was not solved when she and Mitch came into financial wealth. Her physical needs are met, but emotional and personal scars remain. Her husband is a good man and I have always liked Mitch. They have had trouble in their marriage, but so have many Christian couples. That's why we go to the Lord for help. The Lord is the only one who can take our past pain and show how to use it for good—not to drudge it up and use it as a tool to hurt other people. I do hope and pray Helen can find the inner healing she needs to show love to others and not seek ways to hurt them.

CHAPTER FOUR

Hosea
"Bubba"

Hosea Elisha Douglas, Jr. (Bubba) was the first-born son of my parents. Of course, he was Dad's favorite son. By the time you finish reading about him you will think that he is just about perfect. He is.

Bubba was born in poverty, just like all the others. However, he was born at a time when Dad was between jobs. He came out healthy and happy. Mom said he was a happy baby, but a stubborn one. He would use one hand to slide himself across the floor instead of crawling. Mom said he learned to walk quickly and he went exploring once he did.

My brother was alert and smart. He discovered a fascination for nature early on. Bubba actually made a lot of the things that he played with. He was an avid reader and loved my dad's old *Popular Mechanics* magazines, which gave him all sorts of ideas. Bubba built his own kite because we didn't have the money to buy one. He gathered a couple of sticks, some old newspapers, some of Mom's string, flour, water, and rags from old clothes. He made it, and it flew. A store-bought kite would not have done any better.

He was very enterprising and this led to many things he was able to do that the rest of us could not. Bubba asked Dad if he could sell Grit papers. Once he got them, he wasted no time selling them. He made enough money to purchase a scout's knife with many blades. With this knife, he carved out a car from wood Dad had in his shed. A car out of wood! It was a major thing.

He and my brother Larry went to Dad once and asked if they could raise rabbits to sell. Bubba had been reading about how to raise them, how to build a rabbit hutch, and where to sell them. Dad agreed and off he went. It was a lot of work, but they didn't mind doing it. They were able to sell all of the rabbits, but when the last one was gone, Dad told them that it was enough.

Bubba worked on anything he could find to work on. Dad had an old broken lawn mower in the shed so he began work on it. After a few days of cleaning it with gasoline and brushes and replacing parts, he was able to start it and Dad was amazed. Bubba also fixed an old broken radio. He got some copper wiring he found and a metal peg. My brother wrapped the copper wire around the peg and put it inside the radio. He realized that a few tubes inside the case needed to be replaced and somehow figured it all out. Before we knew it, he was listening to his radio beside his bed.

Bubba liked to hunt and fish. Dad used to take Bubba and Larry with him. They would hunt rabbit, squirrel, and deer. He didn't have a gun at first, but when Dad got a new shotgun, he handed the old one down to Bubba. As soon as Bubba got it, he grabbed a rag and some 3-in-1 oil and cleaned it up. He was a good hunter, but an even better fisherman. We all used bamboo poles until we were able to get rods and reels. Although Dad bought his first ones, as soon as Bubba had a job he bought his own. He bought his own fishing boat, too. Once he moved away, he gave the boat to Dad.

Bubba was a good athlete. I have never known many guys who were good at every sport they tried, but he was. The thing I remember the most was his basketball skills. He and some friends put together a team and played recreational basketball. Bubba rarely came out of the game.

They couldn't afford to take him out. He was that good. He was a strong swimmer, but he almost died swimming in the Gulf of Mexico. All of our family, along with my Aunt Dee and cousin Andrew, went to the beach on the Gulf of Mexico one summer. He got out too far and began to sink. As he gasped for breath, my dad, mom, aunt, and cousin formed a line hand-in-hand and reached a long tree branch to him. None of them were strong swimmers, but together they managed to get him back safely. I was numb, afraid, and lost as I watched him out in the ocean and thought of the possibility that I would lose him. Once they got him to safety, I cried with relief.

Bubba was well-liked in school. I wouldn't call him popular, but other boys liked him. He was friendly, outgoing, honest, smart, and an overall guy's guy. He hung out with his friends on weekends and usually came back with something he bought with the money he managed to save. Many of the guys he went to school with lived near us, but his best friend was Henry Hanson. They were both tall, funny, and athletic. Henry really became a part of our family because of Bubba. Dad took him hunting with them all the time and managed to get Henry a Beagle puppy from someone he worked with. Henry's dad died early in Henry's life, so I guess he looked to our dad as a father figure. He and Bubba were almost inseparable.

Bubba and Larry would go to the movies with a lot of the guys who lived nearby. Henry had a rich aunt named Ruby and she bought him anything that he asked for. He asked her to buy him an old white panel van. The truck had a tire well in the bottom of it which would hold two or three people. Once they learned that, Henry would pick everyone up and put some of them in there to get into the drive-in theatre free. They would then take that money to buy their popcorn, cold drinks, and so on.

Bubba took drafting class in high school, and was a straight A student in it. His instructor told him about an engineering firm looking for a draftsman so he applied and got in while he was still in high school. He saved his money and asked Dad to help him find a car to purchase. Dad found a 1956 Chevy. The paint needed a little work, but other than that, it looked good. He began taking everyone to school. Soon, though, it started giving him mechanical problems. Bubba had always assisted Dad with working on his cars, so he knew a little. However, it came to a point where he could no longer get it to run right. He then did something you rarely saw him do. He cried. Dad and Mom talked about it and decided to buy him a car. They bought him a white 1963 Studebaker Lark. It was sharp!

Bubba graduated with honors from high school. He went to the local college majoring in (big surprise) engineering. He was doing very well with his grades, but he came home from school and work one day and told Dad and Mom that he was joining the Marines. Bubba never made a major decision without first doing a lot of research and giving it a lot of thought. He told them that when he got out he would be able to go to school and buy a home on the G.I. Bill and he could be saving money. Bubba convinced them that it was the right decision and ended up in Vietnam after boot camp. He also had Dad drive him down to New Orleans to purchase a red Fiat Spyder convertible. This was the only one in Monroe because New Orleans had the only dealership in Louisiana at that time.

We were all concerned about his time in the war, but he kept letters and photos coming to us to let us know how he was doing. When he got back home, he let us know that he had been chief scout for Marine Corp Intelligence. You see, he found out that he had a photographic memory. This is why he did so well in school without studying much. He memorized the places he needed to plot and came back and plotted them. Hosea was the first scout that had been able to go out without his maps. They were angry at him for doing it at first, but when they realized that everything he plotted was exactly as he said it was, they insisted he not take the maps.

We didn't know this while he was in Vietnam, but once home, he told us how he had almost been killed. He and another Marine had fallen asleep at a deserted bunker. They both were awakened by other Marines capturing Viet Cong rebels who were nearby.

Bubba went back to college. He told Mom that the reason he dropped out the first time was because everyone dressed better than he did and he was humiliated. Bubba learned to dress well this time. He'd get dressed, hop in his Fiat, and go for relaxing drives. About the time he was home, the movie *The Graduate* had come out. This is something to tell. Dustin Hoffman drove that red convertible and he and my brother looked amazingly alike. People actually thought he was Dustin Hoffman!

Bubba went to work at a much larger engineering firm while he was in school. It was Ford, Bacon, and Davis. He was a draftsman at first, but once he received his degree, he became an engineer and he was a major player for his company. Bubba got laid off several times and finally tried some other types of work. He went back to school to become a CPA. He finished that too. Did I mention he graduated with honors in college?

He eventually bought several cars; one after the other: Dodge Charger, Dodge Challenger, and an AMC Javelin. Bubba and Mom got into a big argument and she told him to get out. She later apologized, but he kept packing. He purchased a small wood-frame house two streets down from them. He began remodeling it. Of course, it was very nice when he finished.

Bubba never dated much, but at the request of his friend Henry, he agreed to a double date with Henry's girlfriend's best friend. She was a bit nerdy and initially he wasn't that interested in her. She turned into a butterfly, however, and they became steady. They dated for about six years, and then were married. She became pregnant soon after they were married. They weren't really prepared for a child, but nonetheless, happy about it or not, they had a daughter.

His wife has three degrees and now works as a nurse. They moved to Plano, Texas and have done very well. They never gave away anything they wanted to get rid of. I don't know how they did it, but they always managed to find some way to sell everything; even before the days of e-Bay and Craig's List. He and Millicent have always been good about saving money.

As you can see, Hosea never gave Dad and Mom any trouble. He always went to church and was respectful to everyone. I must say that he was not very tolerant toward priests that were arrogant, loud, gay, or sermon readers instead of speakers. When any of the above was in the pulpit, he would get up and walk out. About thirty years ago he had gone to visit Dad and Mom and while outside the kitchen window, he heard my mom saying bad things about his daughter. He went home, never to go see them again. He harbored that resentment and anger all these years, and didn't attend either parent's funeral. To this day, he has little to do with the rest of his family. I've made an effort by going to his house and phoning him, but he doesn't come to the door nor does he return or answer my calls. I would love to spend time with him, if he'd allow it.

Throughout his life he has done things for and with all of his brothers and sisters. He loved Dad, but never cared for Mom after that one incident. He was close to my older brother Larry and my younger brother Mike. I believe he really loved our sister, Pat, too. He liked Helen at one time but the last time they spoke, he told her that all he needed was his wife and his child. He never allowed any of his brothers or sisters to use vulgar speech or gossip in his home. He eventually stopped doing things with everyone.

That one day when Mom loaded Dad's shotgun to kill him affected him greatly. He was genuinely afraid. Bubba ran out of the house and ran far away in the yard. I think he finally got tired of all the dysfunction he witnessed and I am certain that he was tired of remembering the abuse and neglect he went through. Perhaps shutting us all out is his way of disassociating from that time in his life. Bubba still attends church regularly and has those traits of honesty and integrity. It is a pretty safe bet that he learned lessons from all we went through and wanted a better life for his family. He got it.

CHAPTER FIVE

Larry

Mom said that Larry learned to walk and talk very quickly. I guess you could say he was extremely focused, and his story will show it. Even as a baby, when Larry spotted something he wanted, he wouldn't give up crawling until he reached it. The poverty we all lived in didn't keep him from having a healthy appetite, however it did keep him skinny.

There are many funny stories told about Larry's childhood, and I'll share a few so you can paint a picture in your mind of this brother of mine. Before indoor plumbing, we had to use the hen house for our bathroom. One day Larry had to do number two, so he went out to the hen house with some newspapers. It just so happened that we had a rather large red rooster and boy, he was mean. No sooner had Larry got his pants down, the rooster started at him. It scared Larry so badly that he jumped up before he could do his business and took off running with his pants around his ankles. Poor Larry was yelling and crying for his momma to help him. He ran that way all the way to the house.

As I mentioned earlier, Dad made many of the toys that my older brothers and sisters played with out of wood. Once he made a little cart that was supposed to be a sort of car. Larry loved to play with it. It had two handles like a wheel barrow. When Bubba wasn't around to push Larry in it, he just pushed it himself, making car noises as he raced around. He would be so focused on running fast and having fun that he wouldn't stop to use the bathroom. Mom would stop him when she saw either the ground or his pants all wet. Focus.

When Larry was a little boy the family had a horse named Smokey. When Smokey got near to the fence, Larry got excited. Larry couldn't pronounce "Smokey" so he would call out, "Cokey! Cokey!" All of my uncles and aunts called Larry "Cokey," even into his adult years. If I wanted to get even with him for something he said or did to me, I would wait until a lot of his classmates or friends were around and I would call him "Cokey." Of course this would embarrass him and he would turn his head to survey the room to see how many people heard me say it. But then he'd crack a smile.

Larry was a stubborn little boy. When Mom sat him down to teach him how to write, he would consistently pick up the pencil with his left hand. Mom would slap his hand and place the pencil in his right hand, but as soon as she did so he would switch it back into his left hand. As hard as she tried, my mom could not get him to write with his right hand. He ended up having a beautiful handwriting—with his left hand.

My brother was not smart in school. I believe he was intelligent, but two things kept him from making good grades: focus and fear. While his teachers presented their lessons, Larry liked to look around at the birds and the squirrels in the trees. His focus was misplaced. Secondly, he feared failure and the wrath that would come from Dad when he did fail. This fear stayed with him always and affected the joy he should have had in life. He was shy throughout elementary and junior high.

We were so poor that most of what we ate were starchy foods. Mom cooked beans and rice for just about every meal until she and Dad become financially stable. Given that fact, all of us had gas constantly and that gas had to go somewhere. My dad amazed me because he knew the smell of the odor of each child when this happened and would immediately order us out of the room until it subsided. I'm afraid Larry had the worst and did it the most. Whenever he would excrete his gas, Dad would yell out, "D@#*! That had to be Larry! Boy, get out of the room until you get rid of that!"

Larry would get out and then come back quickly. Sometimes he came back too quickly and it would start all over. The saddest times were when Dad would warn him several times, but Larry didn't want to miss too much of the television show he was watching. His hurry to come back would cost him.

As I said before, Larry's life was shrouded with fear—many different kinds of fear. One of his worst fears as a child was fear of the dark. One time, Dad made Mom put him out on the front porch until his gas subsided and, even though she left the porch light on, Larry cried and begged to come back in with a promise he wouldn't do it anymore. But Dad was cruel. He not only would not let him come back in, he got up and turned the light off, making Larry even more afraid. My brother screamed even louder and his crying intensified. As small as I was (about eight years old), I understood that this was not right!

Often people who carry high levels of anxiety and fear struggle with wetting the bed at night. Larry was a bed-wetter. Dad would use the belt on him for doing it, but Larry couldn't stop. Dad's beatings made it worse and it was a cycle that would not be broken through more beatings. He remained a bed-wetter until he was a senior in high school.

As I said, this brother of mine was very funny. When everyone in the room was frowning, he would manage to do or say something that would make everyone laugh...even Dad! This went on in some of his classes in school. If his teachers got onto him for something he did wrong, he would end up making them laugh.

Of all the brothers, Larry loved to work more than anyone. He especially loved to help Dad work on cars. As a junior in high school, he got a job at a very large and busy local grocery store called "Hensley's." Mr. Hensley really liked Larry because he worked so hard and was great with the customers. By this time, black people were able to be waited on in the stores just like white people. The black people loved Larry, mostly because he made them laugh! When he was cashiering, his line would be the longest because people wanted him to wait on them.

He saved his money, too. Early on in his job, he decided that he wanted a Harley-Davidson motorcycle. Once he had the money, he asked Dad to take him to the dealer because he had the cash to pay for it outright. Dad took him and he came home with a beautiful black and white Sprint 250. They unloaded it off of Dad's truck and he and Dad went over all the things that were vital to driving it. Once they did, Larry jumped on it and rode as if he had always known how to ride. Dad was impressed! It is fair to note that by this time, Larry loved Dad. In fact, he almost worshipped him. When I was about twenty-three years of age, Dad told me outside his house that the one thing he liked about Larry is that he would talk to Dad. He asked his opinion whenever he needed it.

Once he started to work, Larry bought his own clothes. This is a young man who really knew how to dress. He and a friend of his, Wayne Salsbury, would go to town and shop in the most hip of the clothing stores for young men. These were expensive stores, too. J.C. Penney, Sears, and the other stores weren't good enough for him. He also had his hair cut with a razor. This, too, was expensive, but he didn't care. Larry had a very nice appearance. I hadn't mentioned this before, but Larry was handsome, with perfectly white and straight teeth. He was a dentist's dream patient. Eventually he got acne, but sought out a dermatologist and paid for the treatments himself. even though the doctor didn't have to do much, Larry cared about how he looked.

Larry knew he wouldn't make a good college student. Mom was going to put the money away for him to go to college, but he told her not to waste her money. He told her that he wasn't smart enough to finish college. Bubba was in the Marines by this time so Larry decided rather than be drafted, he would enlist in the Marines as well. That is exactly what he did. Larry was only seventeen when he graduated from high school and had to have Dad and Mom sign a release in order to get him in. They didn't want to, but hesitantly signed. This was a big mistake! Larry always lived in fear and a man like that did not belong in live combat. It would eventually take its toll!

Hosea got home from boot camp about two weeks before Larry went in. Hosea didn't do well in boot camp. In fact, it took him far longer to complete it than it should have because he fell and busted a knee cap. Anyway, he shared the stories of his experience to Larry and it was obvious that Larry began to worry a little.

The first day he was in the Marines, they made him write a letter to my parents to let them know how he was. He said in that letter that every Marine was allowed one mistake and that his was signing that agreement to enlist. He did well in boot camp, though. When he finished, he had achieved the rank of Private First Class. This is an achievement that Hosea was unable to obtain. He had been engaged to a very beautiful girl named Evelyn, but he broke up with her while in boot camp because he said he didn't want her waiting on someone who may not make it back from war. She was devastated. Larry always thought of others, even if it was hurtful for himself.

When he got home, he told us that his orders were for Vietnam. My mom broke down and cried. Dad wrote a letter to our congressman to keep him out of Vietnam, but it was useless. He was going. Not only was he going, he was going as a guerilla. (Or as we called it, a "gorilla." Mom called Larry her "little monkey.")

While in Vietnam, Larry earned a Purple Heart, Silver Star, Bronze Star, the Vietnamese equivalent of the Medal of Honor, some medal of gallantry, and was promoted up to the rank of sergeant. He sent audio tapes home to us to let us know what was going on there and we could always hear gunfire in the background. The local newspaper shared articles of his heroics quite often. The band director at my high school would always approach me smiling after he read them. One time, almost his whole company was wiped out and they sent in a group of new recruits fresh out of boot camp. Once the battle began, the new troops froze up and couldn't fire their rifles. Larry ran across the top of the trenches, grabbed each Marine and his rifle, and got the team to start firing. Of course, he was wounded in doing so and received his second Purple Heart. There was a rule in the military at the time that said any military personnel receiving two Purple Hearts had to be sent home. While he was on the plane coming home, he got news that once again his whole company was wiped out. This had a profound effect on him. Vietnam had a profound impact on his life.

As soon as he got home, he went out and bought a Plymouth Road Runner. He was really proud of that car. The first thing he wanted was for every one of us to ride in it. Larry got drunk one night and drove the car right into the ditch just yards from our house. A state police officer drove him home without arrest or ticket. The car was unharmed and he was able to get it out the next day.

He was really proud of the Plymouth, but when Dodge came out with the Challenger, he felt he had to have one. He and Bubba went with Dad to the Dodge Dealership and they each bought one. They got a big discount since they bought two at one time. Every girl in Monroe knew that car.

Larry was looking for love too hard and really didn't know what it was. None of us had an accurate picture of love at the time and looked at everything through the distortion of our at-home experiences. He went through a few engagements until he met a good friend of mine from high school named Annette. They married a short time after meeting.

Larry felt that he had to have everything that our parents had. Dad helped him get a job at Manville and he made good money. He bought a very nice home and began buying everything he thought they needed. Eventually he lost that job and they lost everything they had. He went from job to job trying to find *the* thing that would make him rich. My brother fell for every get-rich-quick scheme that was out there, but never got rich.

He joined the Air Force and retired from it. He then began going from job to job again. My brother began working for Annette's dad, but they made fun of him so he quit. He attempted suicide because of the trouble that he and Annette were having. Larry and Annette divorced, but I know that he never stopped loving her.

Some years later he met and married a girl named Nora. They had two sons and he bought a home. She made pretty good money and he began mud-logging for a very good salary and even drove a company car. Unfortunately they divorced, too. Larry stayed in touch with his sons but couldn't hold down a job anymore. Memories of Vietnam plagued him. While Larry was homeless he traveled all over the U.S. on foot. He hitchhiked for a long time. He went to V.A. Hospitals, trying to get help to deal with his war flashbacks. When Nora was promoted and transferred to Oklahoma, he moved there and got a job. Larry loved his sons and allowed his boys to bring all of their friends over to his house whenever they wanted to. He would cook for all of them.

Larry met another girl and she moved in with him. My brother never stopped going to church as a Roman Catholic. After attempting to commit suicide several times because of the Vietnam flashbacks, he finally succeeded. He moved his girlfriend's car away from the mobile home they lived in and soaked his body and the house with gasoline. Mom said his "little mind" never was right. His body was burned so severely that we had to find medical records to identify him. He died in 1993 at the age of forty-four. Now what I am about to tell you may sound unreal, but is absolutely true. Everything in that mobile home was burned except for his Bible and ALL of his photographs of his children. In fact, there was no smoke damage to them at all.

Larry's funeral was sad. The casket had to be kept closed because he was so disfigured. The funeral home owners told us that we did not want to see what was in there. His youngest son kept jumping up on his casket, crying and telling us he wanted to see his daddy. My dad kept hugging him and talking to him in an effort to console him. It did no good. Not long after my dad passed away, Curtis shot and killed himself at age twenty-five. I could not attend the funeral for two reasons: (1) He looked EXACTLY like his father and (2) He was just too young to die.

Larry was the only child of my parents who was never at odds with any of his brothers or sisters. He and Hosea were very close for most of their lives. They drifted slightly when it was clear that they were not interested in the same things in life. He was always very close to Pat. She'd cry and say that he felt that it was his duty to torment her. It was all in fun and she realized that. I still miss him and I wish he hadn't lived such a sad life. He needed help that he never got.

CHAPTER SIX

Karen

My sister Karen was born in 1950 during a time when Dad was job-hopping and no one knew where the next meal would come from. Karen was born with crooked legs that would prevent her from standing and walking. The brace she wore looked like the rocker from a rocking chair. Both shoes were attached to it and spread out. I can't imagine her difficulty as an infant and a toddler, not to be able get around well enough to play like other children—especially with four older siblings playing all around.

Karen was an overly shy child. Actually, she was an introvert. I am certain this was borne out of fear of our parents. I have never seen a small child who was abused be labeled as "outgoing." Timid and introverted are common characteristics for children experiencing abuse and neglect. She was quiet, didn't really play much, and didn't move around quickly. She hung on to her dolls as if they were saving her from something. In her mind, they probably were. I am sure she pretended they loved her. After all, she wasn't feeling any love from anyone else.

In grade school, Karen made friends easily. I cannot remember too many years that she didn't have a best friend or friends that she went to visit or that visited her at our house. I could almost name them all. They were generous to her, too. Her friends shared their candy, toys, and anything else they had with her.

Outside of the abusive times, Dad seemed to spoil her. He bought her things that he had never bought for the other two girls. I remember him buying her a "Four Seasons" album one time. I was really jealous and confused. He hated the music that his children listened to so why spend money on this? He was bound to hear it!

I realized over time that Dad had an unhealthy affection for Karen. He touched her in ways she didn't like. She fought him off, but he was bigger and her fights didn't stop his advances. He used to laugh because Karen had a very thin hair brush with a sharp back edge to it that she used to hit me and my brothers with when we started bothering her. One day, Dad was bothering her in a way she didn't like so she hit him across the top of his head with it. He didn't laugh that time. He said, "D*@! Karen, don't you hit anybody else with that brush!" My brothers and I laughed because then he knew what it felt like to be hit with her weapon.

Karen was smart in school. Of course, she always did her homework and I know that made a difference. I believe her teachers liked her, and how could they not? She was quiet in class, she was always at school, and she made good grades. She graduated with honors.

Karen didn't date much in high school just as no one else had. She did, however, do a lot of things with her friends. They went to the movies and shopping together. Many of them came over to our house and sometimes did homework with her. She read constantly. No one in our family read like she did. Karen always checked out the maximum number of books the library would allow. She read them all and read them quickly, retaining everything in her sharp mind.

Karen was a very sensitive girl who wore her feelings on her sleeve. She is still that way to a certain extent. Like all of the Douglas children, she had no real concept of what a healthy boy-girl, man-woman loving relationship looked like. I guess she was like me in that she believed what she saw in the movies and on television was the way it was supposed to be. She was smart enough to realize that what she witnessed at home certainly wasn't the way it was supposed to be.

After high school, Mom paid for her to go to college. She entered Northeast Louisiana University in Monroe, Louisiana. It had been a state college that had grown large enough to reach university status. Karen took courses in a two-year business program. She began working at a very large CPA firm in Monroe. Karen made a lot of friends there very quickly. She was a hard worker and strived for perfection. They really didn't pay her very well, but she managed to purchase much better clothes than she had been accustomed to and saved money for a down-payment on a new automobile. Dad took her to the dealership that was owned by "Uncle Buddy," one of Dad's life-long friends. His name was Russell Hart. I think I'm the only one of Dad's children that called him "Uncle Buddy." Karen made very good grades in college and now she could have some of the freedom that she had longed for. She left the CPA firm and has been working for attorneys ever since.

She began picking up her high school friends and going to bars. Karen used to act like she was drunk so that she could get away with falling into boys and get their attention. It worked. She got their attention. Karen, to me, was not a pretty girl, but some of the family in-laws thought otherwise. She had a good figure and I am sure that dressing nicely helped her appearance. Pat told Mom that Karen had confided in her that she had the urge to have sex. Pat told her not to even think like that. Eventually, she did have sex and got pregnant. The guy was wild and didn't care much for her. He would not marry her so she was on her own.

Still living with Dad and Mom, she gave birth to a son.

This was her only child. About the time he was to be born, she began to date a hairdresser that had worked for Vidal Sassoon in New York. His name was Vincent, but he went by the name of "Mr. Vincent." He did seminars on hairdressing around Louisiana and worked in a small shop on the North side of Monroe. She liked him, but he was much older than she was. He came to our house and met everyone. Vince was very outgoing. When Karen's son was born, the nurse asked if he was the father and he started to say yes, but he saw Dad coming down the hall and decided not to.

There began to be questions about him and Dad disliked him immensely. Finally, Karen left home with her toddler, moved into an apartment, and married Vincent. I never liked the guy and neither did Bubba. My brothers Larry, Mike, and Rob attended the wedding, which was officiated by a Justice of the Peace. He used my brothers and my sister. Little Paxton, Karen's son, was totally confused and it was suspected that this guy was beating on him. I do know that when Karen returned home after working eight hours, she had to take care of her son as well as get Vincent's dinner ready. He expected her to have his dinner on the table when he came in for work. It didn't matter what her needs were or the child's needs were. In his mind, he came first.

Finally, Karen left him. This was an excellent idea. Dad and Mom picked her and Paxton up and collected their things. Karen went back home to live with my parents and never left there nor married again. She devoted her whole life to her son and is still doing that. Karen believed in buying him only the best clothing. He wore designer labels, even as a child. With my parents' help, she put him through a private school. They also helped raise him. For all practical purposes, my dad became his dad and his Uncle Mike, my younger brother, was his hero and friend.

I feel I was close to Karen at one time, but I lived in

many places, so I didn't have a great relationship with any of my siblings. She and Pat had children the same age so they did a lot together with their children. They shopped together, went out to eat together, went to the movies together, and had family outings together. Karen is a religious Roman Catholic, just as Pat and Mom were. She says her rosary, reads prayer books, and attends mass on Sundays and all the holy days.

I admire that Karen looked after her Dad and Mom when they could no longer do it. All Mom ever did was yell at her and criticize her. Dad abused us. Yet, she bought groceries, cleaned the house, painted the house, and did whatever else they needed her to do. My dad told me that she had been very good to them. When he got too old to drive, Karen took him where he wanted to go.

After Mom passed away in October of 2014, Karen was left alone, with the exception of a brother who would soon have to leave my parents' house. She packed everything up and called each one of us to pick up what we had given to our parents over the years. Karen planned the funeral and had the paperwork for the estate drawn up. She sold Dad and Mom's belongings and found the realtor to sell the house. She did all of this with the written consent of all of her siblings. Mom's wishes were to sell the house and divide the money between the children. This left Karen without a home. I asked her if she was moving in with her son and his wife in Baton Rouge, but she said she wouldn't be welcomed. Isn't that something!? He, along with my brother Mike, bled my mom dry. My mom never questioned their requests for money to cover this or that emergency or one thing or another that came up. Mom had thousands of dollars in her savings. When they showed up with something new and expensive (like a boat), Mom never asked for an accounting of the money she'd given to cover their "emergency." Karen sacrificed for her son for all of her life. Even though she can't stay with him now, my brother Mike rightly allowed her to move in with him.

Karen's hopes are to get enough money to put a down payment on her own house. Two of my nephews said she could have their parents' share of the money from the sale of the house. My wealthy sister, Helen, said she needed her share. All I know is I've yet to see any accounting of what happened to my parents' money from the sale of their things after Mom passed. It isn't uncommon for abused children—especially those who have lived in poverty—to have distorted views when it comes to hoarding money and lying about financial matters. I've heard there was no money in the bank when Mom died, yet when I went to Louisiana for my mom's funeral, my sister Helen had a new Cadillac, Karen had a new Honda, my brother Rob had a new Dodge Challenger, and my brother Mike had his whole house renovated. I was told that they had to sell all of Dad's shop tools to pay for the utilities. (I happen to know that Mike got most of them some time ago.)

CHAPTER SEVEN

Mike

At this point, I should be writing about me since I am next in line by age. However, if I wrote the chapter about me here I risk the possibility of you tearing up the book and sending hired assassins to take me out. Believe me, it is THAT BAD!

Mike was born completely healthy and happy. He was a very active baby and toddler according to Mom. He learned to walk pretty quickly. I guess it was so he could begin getting into things early.

In his preschool years, he and I would sit at the front screen door and have wild conversations. The Louisiana Training Institute is a boy's reform school. Some of their property was across the street from our house. This is where their cows grazed every day. As soon as we got up from our afternoon nap we sit at the front door and look at the cows. We would point to a cow and lay claims on it as if it were really ours. Then Mike would begin telling me stories about the things he did when he was a man. He owned cattle and drove tractors. Mike owned more land than the mind could imagine. When he was a man, he was very tall and very strong. He owned trucks, too. He didn't own just a few trucks, but at least one hundred, and he would let the guys that worked for him drive all of them except for his favorite red one. He also cut down trees like Paul Bunyan. Mike had a wife when he was a man. Their house had one hundred rooms in it and an indoor toilet. They were rich.

To say Mike had an active imagination would be an understatement. He loved watching westerns on T.V. My brother would get really excited and worked up whenever there was a fight scene. He would begin punching the air with his fists and get giddy as he cheered his favorite heroes on. Mike became all those characters he saw on the westerns. Those same barrels that we had barrel races on became his horse during the day when the older siblings were in school. He found a piece of rope and attached it to the front of the barrel. This was the horse's bridle. If the barrels were unavailable, the saw horses that Dad had made out of wood were a suitable replacement. He would just put the bridle on the sawhorse and hit its rump with his hand. He had some very fast horses and was able to catch the bad guy every time. Mike was the singing cowboy. His favorite thing to sing was "I'm just a lonesome cowboy!" Mom laughed every time she heard it.

Once our baby brother was born, Mike and I were no longer close. He loved that baby. Once Rob started walking, Mike hung around him all day long. Those two remained inseparable for years. We'll talk more about that later on. Once I started school, he would take our baby brother from house to house in the neighborhood and tell the housewives that he and his brother were hungry and ask for something to eat. The neighbors would always give them donuts or cookies. Mike and Rob were full before they had lunch. One of the neighbors finally called Mom to let her know what was going on. As I said, Mike loved that baby and always looked out for him. He was tenderhearted. In spite of the neglect and abuse he received at the hands of my parents, he was crazy about both of them.

My younger brother was a bed-wetter. He remained one through the eighth grade. I used to have to share a bed with him and every morning I would wake up in his urine. Sometimes I would wake up during the night just as he was wetting the bed. The best I could do is try to get as far to the edge of the mattress to avoid sleeping in it. It was usually in vain. I don't know if it was my complaining about having to lie in his urine or if my parents just felt bad for me, but I eventually got my own bed. This condition could have been brought on by the fact that he had juveniele diabetes, but I don't really know. I felt sorry for Mike because Dad would hardly ever give him any spending money the few times he gave it to everyone else because he knew Mike would buy something sweet with it.

Mike loved school. The thing he loved most was all those other little boys he could play with. He was very outgoing and made friends quickly despite how poor and how shabbily dressed he was (holes in the knees of his jeans, torn pockets, and missing buttons on shirts). Mike's average grades were consistent. He wasn't stupid. By the time he started school in the first grade I was in the second, and had earned a reputation for being a "bad dude." A second grader named Tommy Strickland hit Mike one day on the playground and some of my classmates ran to me to tell me. They pointed out where Tommy was and I beat him up. From that point on, no one was willing to touch Mike.

He liked all the arts and crafts he made in elementary school. Mike brought them home as if they were trophies and shared them with Dad and Mom. One year, they made sail boats out of cardboard. A friend of his named David Daigle (the son of a wealthy man Dad knew well) came home with him. The teacher told them to put foil on the boats and they would be waterproof enough to sail in the water. Mike had no idea what foil was, but he thought varnish was foil. He put varnish on his and David's boats. I had been elsewhere and when I got home I went to the back yard where they were sitting waiting on the "foil" to dry. I told him that it wasn't foil, but varnish. He told me it was the same thing. I then told him that the boats would never dry and never float. They ended up throwing them away. He was angry at me for disappointing him and his friend and for making him look stupid. However, he got over it quickly. He knew I would always take up for him at school. Mike could be incredibly naïve. One time Dad brought all of his sons (except Rob) fishing in the boat. It was Mike's first time to fish from a boat. A dog barked off in the distance and the sound traveled across the water.

I said, "Did you hear that dogfish?"

Mike got excited and said, "Hey Daddy, did you hear that dogfish?"

My two older brothers were smiling from ear to ear. Dad said, "That wasn't a dogfish. Dale, you ought to cut that #%@* out!"

My brothers laughed. Mike was angry.

One day when I was in the fourth grade and he was in the third, his teacher brought him to my classroom and called my teacher out to the hall. She lifted up the back of his shirt and revealed bruises and whelps on his back. Then she pulled up the legs of his jeans and revealed the same thing. Some of those whelps had dried blood on them. They called me into the hallway. My teacher asked if I knew how he received them. It seems Mike told his teacher that he got them playing football the day before. It is true that we played football that day, but Dad had beaten us that day, too. Then my teacher pulled up my shirt and jeans and there were the same whelps, cuts, and bruises. We thought they bought our story because I backed Mike up on his story.

That same day, when Dad had been home only a few minutes, a man with a cowboy hat drove up in a green and white Chevy with some kind of writing and what looked like a badge painted on the doors. Mike and I were excited to see him because we thought he was a real cowboy. We started to go over there to meet him, but my mom told us to stay away from there. It turns out that he was a deputy sheriff and he was following up on the report the school called in about two of his little boys having cuts, bruises, and whelps on their bodies. They talked a long time. Dad was pretty quiet that night. The man came back and spoke to Dad again a couple of times but never arrested him. We didn't get beatings for a good while after that.

My younger brother was mischievous. Dad had a truck when we were in junior high and we loved it. One day when Dad got home from work, he showed Mom a bent truck key and a new key he had made while he told her how he bent it and how he had the new one made. He then threw the bent key in the trash can in the dining room. Mike and I paid close attention. When everyone was out of the room, Mike retrieved it while I was the lookout.

Dad and Mom went out of town in Mom's car so my older sisters were in charge. When everyone else was gone away from the house, Mike handed me the key and we got in the truck. He asked me if I knew how to drive it and of course I said I did. I had watched Dad go through the gears so I knew what to do, although I had never done it. I backed the truck out of the driveway and away we drove. We were laughing and having a great time. After a short while, he asked if I would help him learn. I pulled the truck over and we changed places. Then I attempted to teach him. He caught on pretty good. It wasn't great, but he was driving. We went everywhere. The best part about it is that we made it back home without anyone knowing we had driven. We hid the key. Dad and Mom got back Sunday night and no one knew we had driven. Monday morning Dad got in his truck, started it up, shut it off, got out, and came back in the house. Mom asked what was wrong. He told her that someone had driven his truck because he had much more gas than that. Uh-oh! We hadn't thought about the gas! Mom convinced him that it would have been impossible for someone to drive his truck because his keys and her keys were with them out of town. From that point on, Dad kept a sheet of paper in his truck and wrote down the mileage every day. That was the end of that.

Mike was not a pretty child. He had blonde hair and blue eyes. This was far different than his brown-eyed brunette brothers and sisters. I don't really know if the girls thought he was cute or not, but he was certainly interested in them once he was in high school. Our two older brothers didn't really date much in high school, but Mike and I made up for it. It was hard on both of us because we didn't own cars. We couldn't schedule dates on the same night because Mom's car was the only one we could use. When his first steady girlfriend broke up with him, he was heartbroken.

My younger brother was a gifted athlete. He was good at football, basketball, baseball, and especially in track. Mike was a long-distance runner and one of the best in the district. He had a beautiful stride and made it look so easy. Mike won trophies and medals for his efforts. He wanted to be a pole-vaulter, but didn't succeed. Dad bought him a pole and built us a pit, but he wasn't good enough to do it at school.

After he graduated from high school, Mom offered to put him through college, but he told her the same thing that Larry had told her. He said he wasn't smart enough. Mike went to work instead. He got a job at Kentucky Fried Chicken and the franchise owner really liked him. Somehow, he knew he needed a better job. A lady that had helped me find a job through the agency she worked at got him a job at 7-Eleven. Mike did really well there. He worked hard and learned fast. The supervisor loved him and he was promoted pretty quickly. However, he got off of work one night and two guys waited for him in the dark on the unlighted side of the store. They beat him up pretty badly.

Mike didn't want to quit because he had been able to purchase a brand new red Chevy Vega with the money he had saved. Of course, Dad had to sign the note, but he was faithful to make the payments. Finally, he realized that he needed to quit. He turned in his resignation, but the supervisor didn't want to take it. He kept calling our house and asking Mike to meet with him. Mike wouldn't meet with him so finally, he called and told Mike he was coming to our house to talk to him. Dad told Mike he could leave and Dad handled the supervisor. He didn't call back.

The same lady that helped Mike get that job helped him get a job as a journeyman glass fitter. Mike was good at it and all the older guys liked him. He learned fast and got promoted quickly. That job paid him well and his traveling expenses were always paid.

He bought a Plymouth Road Runner and all the girls wanted to ride in it. He dated a girl from another high school and asked her to marry him. She said yes and told her mother. Mike was excited. He shouldn't have been, though. She slept around with a lot of guys. While Mike was serious, she wasn't. She broke things off with him. Mike was hurt. The girl had been working at Burger King and had a friend named Denise that wanted to take Mike from her. She even bought a necklace with his name on it. She began dating Mike and they eventually married. She, too, had a very bad reputation and Mike even knew some of the guys who could validate that. He didn't care. He was in love. One more of my parent's children had no idea what real love was.

Her love for Mike faded. Denise began writing hot checks and finally got arrested for it. Mike called Mom and she gave him the money to get her out of jail and make restitution for all the bad checks she wrote. They had money to pay the bills, but Denise spent the money instead of paying them.

Twenty-three years went by and she was always in question. She would stay out all night or flowers would be delivered to their house when Mike had not ordered any for her. She never had a good explanation for it. At some point, she was staying out until five o'clock in the morning and when Mike questioned her about it she would say, "Oh, Mike! You just don't want me to have any fun!" He asked her if she knew of any man who would allow his wife to stay out all night and not ask her where she had been. She had no answer so he told her she needed to pack up and go. She did. He was heart-broken. Mike grieved her for a long time, but even her own family told him that she was no good and that he could do much better. Her parents told him to forget about her. They finally divorced, but Mike continued to love and grieve for her.

Mike is a tattle-tale and a brown-nose. He has been like this his whole life. Dad had a strict rule that we were to be home at 10:00 pm on a date night. If I stayed out five minutes later than this, he would yell and scream at me. Mike stayed out until eleven one night and Dad got onto him, but not like he did with me. He asked Mike if he had told him to be home at 10:00 pm, but Mike told him repeatedly that it was eleven. Finally, Dad gave up and they both went to bed. Once in bed, he told Dad that he was wrong and after careful thought it was 10:00 pm after all. Dad was impressed and told Mom how honest Mike had been.

After I had been married for about a year or so, Mike came over to my house. He laughed with us and acted like he really enjoyed visiting. The next day my mom called. She was angry and told me everything my wife and I did and said. We knew the only way she could know this is if Mike had told her. Unbelievably, he showed up at our door the next night. We couldn't believe he would have the gall to do that! I surprised him, though. I let him in. When I did, my wife was angry and went to our bedroom. I let him talk but I never said a word. He finally got tired of the silence and left. He never came back again.

When I got married, I bought my house and furnishings myself. I paid for my car myself. My dad and mom paid for Mike's wedding, his furniture, his appliances, and everything else he needed for his home once he was married. If he made a bill, Mom paid it.

The glass fitter's union went on strike so Larry got him a job as a mud-logger. He was making more money so he never went back to glass fitting. He began to buy new trucks, cars, boats, shotguns, and other expensive things. Mom paid his bills when he got laid off at first, but then she just paid his bills period. He used to sit in her den and tell us all to our faces that nobody paid his bills. My siblings and I would all just look at one another. We knew the truth. He used Mom up.

He loved to hunt and fish like my Dad, so he was Dad's second favorite son for a long time. Once Dad realized just how much Mike was taking advantage of Mom, he had no use for him. He would mow and trim Dad's yard when Dad got too old, but he expected to be paid for it. Mom expected it, too. If I or anyone else mowed it, we did it just because they asked us to.

At Christmas, he gave Dad and Mom one gift for both of them. He gave them a twenty-dollar bill to share. That's it. He was usually out in the woods hunting Christmas Eve and Christmas Day. Mike would tell the lady he worked for that he needed to be off several weeks or so when deer hunting season opened. During that time he had no income, yet his bills kept getting paid.

When I was able to start buying things for myself, I

wouldn't wear anything but Polo, Nautica, Tommy Hilfiger, Izod, and other designer and name-brand clothing. I noticed Mike began doing the same. Guess who paid for all that? He was talking loud and boasting one day in my parent's den about purchasing a Nautica jacket for $75, but the original price was $350. I had been wearing Nautica for years and knew that they didn't make a jacket such as he was describing, but I didn't say anything. It hurt Mom's feelings that he said that. I think it was because she thought that she was sacrificing the things she wanted in order to pay his bills while he went out and spent money on expensive things for himself. I don't blame her.

When my dad was in the hospital dying, Mike avoided the hospital and instead busied himself repairing things at Mom's house. When I got to Mom's house one day to take a shower, he began running his mouth, talking loudly about the fact that he couldn't do anything for Dad, but he could help Mom by repairing some of the things she needed repairing. I hadn't said a word to him—he was talking to be heard by others.

At Dad's funeral, I overheard Mike and Paxton planning how they were each going to ask Mom for money. They didn't think anyone heard or saw them in their little huddle, but I did. They got their money, too.

Mike stabs me in the back all the time, but as soon as he sees me he comes up and hugs me. I've come to understand that is just how it is for him. His mind is weak, and he has replaced our mom's role in his life with our sister Helen. Helen manipulates him to do or say anything she wants. He was one of the first to come to her aid when she and I had that big argument about her telling my past to Lynn. Then, when I went to the funeral home to see Mom, he ran up and hugged me and Lynn and asked how we were doing. If it had not been my mom's funeral, he would have received something besides a hug. At one point during the viewing, he told me that I should have been there while Mom was in the hospital. I couldn't be there because no one told me she was sick. Mike knew this and couldn't even look me in the eye as he said it. I'm sure he boasted to his new mother, Helen, that he told me off, but the behavior was cowardly.

I often asked the question, "What will Mike and Paxton do once Mom is gone?" Mike is worried sick about how his bills are going to get paid. He is scrambling to find answers, and aligning with Helen is not going to yield the results he desires. As children, we have to depend on our parents for our needs (even if they aren't properly met). But at some point, we become responsible for our decisions and actions and must mature into adults who contribute positively to society. If we don't mature, we end up in a never-ending cycle of poverty. Poverty of character, poverty of relationships, and poverty of life. Mom's enabling of the behavior never forced Mike to mature into an adult. He's going to have to do it on his own. God is waiting to help him, if Mike ever decides to ask. Mike stopped going to church after he got married. That was a day that he had off so he could sit at home and get drunk. That is what he did. In the late 1980s he was in a bad traffic accident and killed another man. Mike was in a coma for about a month. He said that while he was in that coma, he and God had a long talk. For a brief time he said he was in church every time the doors opened. That didn't last long.

He is still a Roman Catholic and lives very close to a church. He has no idea what God is really about and acts like he doesn't need Him. Mike is lost, and he is miserable. All those things that he bought and Mom paid for have not brought him any happiness. I feel that the reason that he brown-nosed Dad and Mom was in order to stop the abuse. As a child, you could hardly blame him for that. Children just want it to stop, they don't care how. But once the abuse stopped, he could never stop brown-nosing. He was getting everything he asked for. He has a relationship with Helen and Karen, but that is about it. He once had a relationship with Hosea and Rob, but they are gone. He thinks he will always have a good relationship with Karen's son, Paxton, because they are just alike. He is wrong. Mom is gone and unless he has something to offer Paxton, Paxton will have no use for him. Helen will at some point find him useless as well. God is there waiting, but Mike thinks he can outsmart anyone, including God.

Good luck with that.

CHAPTER EIGHT

Rob
"Jube"

Rob is my baby brother, the last-born of my siblings. He was a large baby and very healthy when he came into the world. I cannot say the same about my mom. She almost died giving birth to him. Mom began to hemorrhage while in labor, brought on by malnutrition. Mom was extremely weak and had not been able to afford vitamins or see a physician regularly while she was pregnant. I still remember the day Dad brought Mom and Rob home from the hospital. He opened the back door to the car and there was Mom and Rob lying in the back seat.

Considering who he had been born to, his natural baby-happiness wouldn't last long. Dad played with him when he was an infant and a toddler. He would come home from work and put Rob in his lap and talk to him. There was a character in the comic strip, "Lil' Abner" named Jubilation T. Cornpone. Dad used to sing a song about that character and he gave Rob the nickname Jubilation T. Cornpone, which got shortened to "Jube." From that point on we all called him Jube.

My younger brother Mike adored him and they were inseparable up until about ten or fifteen years ago. I felt an obligation to look out for my two younger brothers as long as I was still at home before starting school.

As has been established, Dad had all of us working in the field to harvest the vegetable crops he planted. No one two years of age or older was exempt. Jube had to help. He was picking okra one time and didn't know any better but to rub his eyes while he was picking. Of course, his eyes began to burn and itch and he started crying. Helen told Mom that he had been rubbing his eyes, so they took him in the house to take care of him. It was almost too dark to pick anymore anyway at this point.

My dad brought home toys for Jube every payday. It wasn't always something expensive or big, but it was always something. The one I remember the most is a red pedal tractor he bought him. I don't remember how old he was, but Mike and I were jealous. We were both too big to ride it, really, but it didn't stop us from getting on it and trying.

As much as Dad spoiled him, Jube was still one of the children, so he was going to get beat just like the rest of us one day. I really didn't expect that day to come so soon. Mom was sitting in her rocker when Dad came home one day and she told him that he needed to whip every one of us because we had all been bad that day. Dad lined us up against the dining room wall from the oldest to the youngest. Yes, that included that baby of two years old. He took off his belt and beat us one by one, while Mom sat there calmly watching and enjoying the show.

After he beat each one of us, he would ask what we had done wrong that day. He didn't ask before the beating. I guess that might not have allowed him to have a reason to beat. He left whelps and bruises on each one of us. When he got done with my younger brother, Mike, I figured he was finished. He wasn't. That no good devil had his hand with the belt raised back and was about to hit Jube.

I was really afraid for Jube so I yelled out, "No!" and ran in front of Jube. I got hit in the face at first, but my action made Dad angry. So he continued to hit me. I didn't care. I just didn't want him to hit that baby. He didn't.

Jube was a smart little boy. Of course, he had seven siblings teaching him words and their meanings without knowing it. He learned well. He did not like starting school, however. The first day of school, I had to take him to his classroom. He had a frightened look on his face when he realized that I was going to leave him there. He began to scream and cry and he ran to me and held on for dear life. Mrs. Black got his hands free and I left him. Jube cried every day for a long while. One day, he decided to run away from school. They found him but called my mom. The principal and the teacher thought that he may have a mental problem and wanted to put him in the class with the mentally challenged children. Mom was angry and told them that they better not even try. Dad called the principal that night and used a very forceful tone with him. They left him in the class and his grades were outstanding.

When he got to the fifth grade, he was tested and evaluated by a lady from the school board. His IQ was in the stratosphere! She began to ask him for the meaning of words and the words got more and more difficult. He knew the meaning of every word. The last word she gave him was "hara-kiri." He said, "Suicide." She laughed and asked how he knew that. He said he didn't know how, but he just knew. The lady called my parents that night and told them that he had set the woods on fire. The school wanted to put him in the "gifted" class in the sixth grade. They allowed it. Jube skipped the seventh grade and went on to the eighth.

When he got to high school, he was very outgoing. Rob had a lot of friends and he often went home with them or they came to our house. His best friends were two brothers who went to our church. They were Mike and Mark Filhiol. They were the three musketeers. Still, my brother Mike and Rob remained almost inseparable. They were always playing together out in the yard. Very often the playing would turn into fighting, but Rob forgave Mike quickly and things went back to normal. When they would play together, Mike would always cheat and Rob called him on it angrily. Before you knew it, they were rolling around on the ground fighting, but Mike would be laughing.

Sometimes Rob would be outside playing quietly by himself when Mike would spot him and head toward him. Mike would put his arm around Rob's shoulder and Rob around his and they would be talking and laughing while they walked. All of a sudden Mike would put his foot out, trip Rob, and throw him on the ground. Rob would almost always say, "Dadgum it, Mike! I'm telling mother!"

Mike would say, "I'm sorry! I'm sorry!" or "What's the matter?" or "I didn't mean to!" Sometimes that would stop Rob's pursuit of Mom and sometimes it wouldn't. If he kept going toward the house, Mike would say, "OK, you little bas@#%^!"

When Mom would open the door and call Mike's name he would say he didn't do anything or it was an accident. It was always funny to me. I'll tell you what wasn't funny to me, though. After Dad stopped beating us, I would get in a fight with Mike and while I had him on the ground, Rob would jump on top of me so that I was forced to fight both of them. After this happened several times, Dad became fiery mad! He got onto both of them for it. Dad told him that it seemed that every time I fought one of them, I had to fight both of them. It was the first time I can ever remember Dad taking up for me.

Mike, Rob, and I began to collect and assemble model cars. Rob was still being spoiled by Dad and Mom so he got many great model cars. Mike or I would usually have to help him put them together. Mike would always find a way to get Rob to give them to him. He would get a bunch of junk or trash together to trade for them. An example of that is the time he gave him two rubber bands, an empty thread spool, a coke cap, a broken pencil, and a used pencil eraser for one of his best cars. If Mike's appeal to him with junk wouldn't work, he would try the sympathy approach. He would start looking all sad and hang his head down. I would go to Rob on Mike's behalf and say, "Why don't you trade with the little fella?" He would usually give in.

All three of us worked at our church one summer and earned money to buy our own school clothes. Mike and I went out on our own, pretty much. Rob went shopping with Mom. The stores in Eastgate Shopping Center were having a sidewalk sale so tables of sale merchandise were outside. Mom said he went from store to store looking and he would tell the salesclerks, "I like these, but first I'm going to see what your competitor has." He was very bright.

Mike would sometimes see Rob coming toward a doorway so he would hurry to get to it first, stand or lean in it, and say, "I'm standing right here all day and if anybody bumps into me I'm going to hit them!" Naturally, Rob would bump into him or he would nudge Rob as he walked past and they would start to wrestle around. They continued that even after Mike got married. It would happen when Rob went to visit him at his house.

Some people are naturally athletic and Rob was one of them. He played football, basketball, and baseball very well. While he was in high school he decided that he was handsome enough to be an actor. He was in school plays and eventually became part of the community theatre. Not only was he a very good actor, he was a good director as well. As I mentioned before, he was outgoing and very popular. Yet, something was wrong. The abuse and neglect took a toll on him. He had always been happy and focused. Then, while in high school, in one year's time, he had several friends die with only a couple of weeks or months between each. He went to every funeral and came home crying every time. Rob would describe how each looked through his tears. This changed him a little. He would be laughing and in a great mood one minute and the next he would be angry and even hostile.

When Rob entered college at Northeast Louisiana University in Monroe, he was pursuing an acting career. He landed every part he ever auditioned for and directed plays in school as well. His photo and stories about him were often in the newspaper. He was hired to do television commercials, which paid pretty well. He didn't stay in college, though. Rob left school with only one year remaining.

In keeping with his almost arrogant personality, he became a radio disc jockey. Rob would call himself, "Your glamour boy!" He said it kept the girls calling and he met and dated a number of them.

From there he had a number of jobs. Mike got him a job working for the glass company that he worked for, but he was let go because one of the bosses said that he played around too much. He was a painter and eventually had his own painting company, but it folded. A friend of his, Jim Kokinos, hired him to sell clothing in his clothing store for a while. Rob was a disc jockey in a very large night club and Mike got him a job with him mud-logging. He left that job to go to Colorado to work for another drilling company and that took him on the road for a while. He hung out with the actor Slim Pickens in Jackson Hole, Wyoming for a while when he was with that company. Rob had worked as a salesman for a tire company, but they really jerked him around so that didn't last. He even worked for a fast food drive-in once. He also worked for a cable and wireless company where he became the regional vice president in Phoenix. There was a lot of job-hopping.

Rob got worried when Mom had her heart attack so he

asked his cable and wireless company if he could go back to a sales job and move to New Orleans. He wanted to be close to home if something happened to Mom. He lived in Dallas a while and came over to my house only once in the short time he was there.

Rob always said that he wasn't going to marry unless it was for money. My baby brother loved money or, I guess I should say, loves money. When he found out that Mom had a large amount of money that she intended to give to Paxton, he called her and told her that he would see to it that Paxton never got his hands on it. He called me and told me the whole story. Mom called right after he did and asked me to take up for Paxton if Rob called, but she wouldn't tell me what she and Rob were arguing about. Rob felt that he should get that money. My baby brother was angry when he found out that Mom was giving so much money to Mike and was paying his bills.

Rob got married when he was nearing his thirtieth birthday. She was a doctor. He got the money he had been looking for. Everyone thought things were going well, but they divorced. He lived with a girl while he was in Colorado, but she eventually went back to her old boyfriend. He was devastated. Again, he married another doctor. Her dad was a pastor and I thought that it might be forever, but it too ended in divorce. Can you see the pattern?

Mike was really the only sibling that Rob was close to for any amount of time. I know that when he was little, my sister Pat used to take him with one of her boyfriends on some of their dates. The guy liked Rob. He and Helen talked a lot for a while but they don't do much of that anymore. In fact, from 1992 until about 2013, Rob and Helen tried to tell everyone how things were going to be done in the Douglas family. He tried to boss all the rest of us around and run our lives and dictate our decision-making. Isn't that something else? He can't even run his own life. How on earth did he expect to run anyone else's? Rob loved his mother. Mom told Helen and me that she was sick of him telling her how much he loved her all the time. I told her that he did and he did. He didn't like my dad too much. Perhaps it was the double-standard of buying him things and the beatings. Dad had always appeared to love him. My dad bought him two cars and signed for him to buy others. He never signed for me to buy one, let alone bought me one. I am the only child he didn't sign for. When Rob decided he wanted to go back to college, Dad paid off his credit card bills so that he could. It was Dad that provided the funds for him to start his own painting business and even gave him his Plymouth van to use. Remember, Dad bought him gifts all the time when he was little.

Dad felt that Rob used him and my mom. They both told me that the times that he lived away he would call all of his friends in Monroe and tell them to meet him at their house when he was going to visit. They said he never went there to visit them because he got drunk with his friends. Both of my parents said he acted like their house was a motel.

Mom said he called her when he was making six figures crying that he owed the IRS a huge sum of money and they were going to put him in jail if he didn't pay. He told her that if she would loan him the money to pay it, he would pay her a set amount every month. She said he did that for a couple of months and then stopped. Mike, Rob, and I once helped Dad paint the house and put up a fence around his back yard. Afterward Dad made the statement that I was the one who did it all. Rob called me all hot and angry and said that Dad said that just to be hateful. I told him that Dad was getting older and he was just forgetful. Rob argued and refuted that statement and started on a rant. I was standing in my kitchen when he called. When I saw that I wasn't going to get in a word edgewise, I laid the phone on the countertop, walked into my living room, sat down in my recliner, and started watching television with my wife. She asked, "What did Rob have to say?"

I said, "He's still saying it. He was ranting so much I couldn't get a word in edgewise so I laid the phone on the countertop. I'll go back in a little bit."

She said, "Oh-h-h-h! Honey!" I waited about thirty minutes, went back into the kitchen, picked up the phone, and he was still going and never knew that I had laid that phone down.

This is extremely sad, but Rob became an alcoholic. He begins drinking whiskey as early as seven o'clock in the morning. He goes on binges for days on end. Rob has come very close to death several times. His wife in Georgia put him in detox once, but he wouldn't stay. Mom talked him into going again about a year ago or so, but he didn't stay that time either. He and his wife split up, and he went to live with Mom. She complained about Rob and said that he would throw up and mess on himself. She had to clean it up. I learned from my sister Helen that he would be so drunk that he would pass out before he made it to his bedroom, and Mom, that little eighty pound woman, would try to pick him up and get him to the bed! My mom told me that he hit my dad in the face a short time before he passed away and she was afraid he was going to hit her too.

Mom died due to a serious infection called C. diff. It is highly contagious and you can get it by handling feces. She got it from cleaning up after Rob. She went into cardiac arrest because the infected blood passed through her heart. He got drunk and missed his mother's funeral. When he went to the funeral home the night before her burial, he had been drinking. He boasted that she had spoiled him all his life and was still doing it when he was fifty-eight years old. Rob was smiling the whole time he said it. It made me sick. I left the funeral home.

Rob was told that he had to be out of the house because it had to be sold per Mom's orders. Rob stayed there for so long Karen thought she was going to have to get a court order to get him out. He finally left but currently I don't know where he is. I don't know if he is going to church. At one time he professed to be Roman Catholic. I have not been the only one to talk to him about Christ, but his refusal to accept Christ all goes back to the number one reason that humans sin: pride. Rob loves alcohol more than he loved his mother and more than he loves himself. He has refused help because he says he knows what he's doing. I worry about him, but you cannot help someone who refuses to listen.

All I can do for Rob is pray. And I do. If you think of it, please pray for him, too.

CHAPTER NINE

Me

Before you begin to read this chapter, I must warn you that this is a very graphic and disturbing chapter. If you cry easily, cannot forgive people for their mistakes, get angry easily, are judgmental, find it difficult to face evil, and don't like hearing the truth, then you need to either shut this book and tear out this chapter or skip over it and go to the last chapter. I do not apologize for what I have written, but have asked and received God's forgiveness for all I am disclosing. Those who know me will certainly look at me in a much different way than they have before. Those who do not know me will see a progressive transformation as they turn the pages. For my sister Helen, this will be a thrill because she has always wanted to know all of my business. This should put her mind to rest. Let's begin. Are you ready?

When my mom was about five or six months pregnant with me, my brother, Hosea, fell out of a moving car. My mom put her right index finger on her lip just below her nose quickly as a sign of disbelief. She attributes my harelip to her making this gesture.

My grandfather on my dad's side was born on the 15th of January. My mom's doctor told her that I would be born on that day as well. Midnight came around and I still wasn't born. Just after midnight, I came into the world wearing a harelip and a cleft pallet. This is the first of nine times that I should have died. Although no one knew it at the time, I also had amblyopia (lazy eye) in my left eye. Papa, my grandfather, wasn't concerned too much with the harelip, but he was shooting out fire from his eyes because I was born on the 16th instead of the 15th. It took him a long time to forgive my mom; as if she had any control over it. I think my dad was ashamed of me and really didn't want me. I'm not sure my mom did either, to tell you the truth.

My mom and I took train rides through the United States trying to find a surgeon who could help me. Finally, a physician in New Orleans did surgery on my lip and closed it up. He took skin from my hip and butt to repair it. My mom said that, because of the way my cleft pallet was, I had a tough time breathing under the gas they administered to me to put me to sleep. When the anesthetic wore off, I came out fighting as if I was afraid of dying. I was just an infant and already I was living in fear. From that point on, according to Mom, I did not want to be out of her sight and I would fight anyone who came near my mom. The nurses and staff at the hospital, however, made me their baby. Mom said I was in somebody's arms or lap the whole time I was at the hospital.

Once we got home, Papa and Maudie wanted to keep me overnight at their house...a lot! My parents allowed it, but I'm not sure why. Maybe the grandparents were just demanding or maybe I would be out of my parents' sight so I was out of mind, too. My grandparents loved me and didn't want anyone to harm me. One time I had been staying at their house for over a week when my Uncle Bill and his children came by. Papa had put me out in the backyard on a blanket with toys so that I could play outside. My cousin, Clifton (Uncle Bill's oldest), ran out the back door, ran up to me, and started taking my toys away. Papa grabbed him up, took off his belt, and beat the daylights out of him. He told Clifton not to ever touch me again or he would kill him. Uncle Bill didn't like that, but he didn't say a word and he treated me with kindness for the rest of his life. In fact, when all my uncles and aunts realized that I was my grandparents' favorite grandchild, they all treated me as if they loved me whether they really did or not.

My parents said that I was an observant child. They said that from the time I came out of the womb, I would look all around me and would stop to stare at something for fifteen or thirty minutes at a time. I have remained one of those people who stares to this day. Whenever anyone in my family was looking for something, I would never say a word, but I would walk straight to where it was. It is fair to point out at this time that before I was two years of age, I already had an incredible memory. This, too, has stayed with me all of my life. I am my family's memory. When there's a discussion about something that happened when we were children, one of my parents or siblings would call me to get the facts of the situation. I still remember clearly things that happened when I was two years of age. I must confess that my short-term memory is slipping a bit, but never has my long-term memory failed me.

I remember that I had my very own dog when I was two years old. His name was Scottie. I used to lay down with him on the floor and fall asleep. When Scottie died, Dad got the shovel and buried him in the back yard. I asked Mom about Scottie when I was about sixteen years old. She swirled around quickly to look at me and said, "How can you remember that? You were only two!" I guess I remember it because of the love the dog and I shared between each other.

I was a quiet child and pretty much kept to myself. It is fair to say that most children are happy when their dad comes home from work, but, even as a toddler, I became tense when Dad got home. It would be unfair to say that he beat someone most of the time once he got home but it certainly seemed that way. Most of the time it was Mom who got beat. When the other children were at school, I sat on the floor watching my mom sweep, mop, cook, iron, wash clothes and dishes, and dust furniture. I really didn't like to have her out of my sight.

When my siblings got home from school, they had pictures that they had colored at school and they had their other school work. They all competed to show Mom what they had accomplished at school that day. I liked looking at the work and I loved seeing all their tools for going to school. They had Big Chief tablet paper with solid and dotted lines, color crayons, paste, compasses, books, and Popsicle sticks. It was fun for me to see them changing out of their good rags to get into their really shabby rags to play in. Mom made them do their homework before they could go out to play so I got to hear her asking questions and explaining their lessons to them. We didn't have a television until after my baby brother was born so this was my entertainment.

At two years of age, I went out with the rest of my family into the field to harvest the crops Dad planted. I was barefoot and hot. The crops were always taller than me, so I was in constant fear of being out of sight from someone, especially when it began to get dark. Also at two years of age, I didn't have a bed to sleep in. I used to have to sleep with one of my older sisters or brothers, but I never knew which one it was going to be from day to day.

After my younger brother was born, I had someone to play with, but no toys to play with. We used anything we could as toys. One day it might be an old lard can or a broken broomstick. It really didn't matter what it was. Anything was acceptable.

I had many childhood fears and some of them I have never outgrown. I'll start with the worst one first. The door to my parents' bedroom was green. It was a solid wood door with the panels cut out. Every house had them, and all the doors in our house were like that. The only two differences in this door were that it was painted green and that my parents slept behind it. I was deathly afraid of that door. You may be thinking that this was crazy, but it wasn't to me. Evil, hatred, beatings, yelling, abuse, and neglect lived behind that door. I would walk fast through the house until I reached this door. Then, I would step very slowly and deliberately to get through it. I didn't go through it unless I had to.

I was afraid of the dark. Because Dad kept us out in the field after dark and, with the crops being taller than me, fear struck me like lightning on a lightning rod. If I couldn't see people or where I was going, I would be alone and I didn't know what moved in the dark. It didn't help that my sister Helen used to scare me with stories of the dark. She loved to try and scare everybody.

For as long as I can remember, I have been scared of closed-in spaces. Again, Helen used to lock me in a room and stand against the door so that I couldn't get out. I was too small to reach the doorknob, so I was just trapped. She would put my head under the quilts and hold it there so that I couldn't get out of that either. I still have this fear.

I was also scared of heights. I felt that every adult was tall. I guess they were compared to me. My uncles used to grab me and lift me up above their heads. They would laugh, but I wouldn't. I was especially scared when they'd sneak up behind me to do it. I used to climb trees, making mental notes of every step I took to get where I was going so that I could make a quick exit if I got too scared.

One of my worst fears involves a combination of the black Catahoula Cur dog we had named Ike and the steps that were on the back and the side of the house. I had a recurring dream that every time I walked by those steps Ike would come out growling and eat me. It was always dark in the dream. I have to explain that Ike loved all of us children and he was our protector. If any of us were outside playing and someone tried to come into the yard, he would get between us and that person and bark and growl and show his teeth. He stood his ground and was immovable. People were afraid of him, but none of us were. He died when someone poisoned him with rat poison in hamburger meat. So why was I scared? It really was the steps that I was afraid of. This is why. When Dad came home from work, he and Mom would sit on those steps while he had a cup of coffee or a glass of ice water, and filed the hoes and spades that were used in the field. He was not ashamed of beating Mom or us at those steps. The steps came to be a symbol of the abuse that was dealt out by my dad.

It will be hard for anyone who knows me to find out that I was afraid of the water, but I was. Dad and Mom would take us to Forsythe Park in Monroe where they had a city swimming pool. Dad bought us something we called "rubber rings" to keep us afloat. They were really made from plastic, but that's what Dad called them so we did too. He wasn't a good swimmer so he never really taught us to swim and we could not afford swimming lessons. I think some of the kids took lessons from the Red Cross, but Karen, Mike, Rob, and I never got to. Here is probably the biggest reason I was afraid of the water, though. Most of the food we ate we grew, hunted, or fished for. Dad used to load all ten of us in his 1951 Studebaker Champion and take us out in the woods where there were plenty of small ponds to fish from. We stood on the bank with earthworms hanging from our cane poles. One day, we were fishing in one such pond that had a large culvert above it. I stood high on that culvert and kept getting closer and closer to the edge until I fell in. The pond was FULL of water moccasins and they were swimming all around me. I did not know how to swim, but my brothers and sisters told me that I was swimming that day. My mom jumped in the water and came to save me. It wasn't very deep, but I didn't know that. This was now the second time that I should have died.

I was afraid of my dad and mom. I thought that one day they were going to kill me. I thought that they would get so mad that they would beat me so severely that I would die. One Saturday, Dad and Mom had been arguing and he slapped her around as usual. He had gone somewhere and while he had been gone, Mom and my sisters loaded suitcases with our clothes in the back of her Oldsmobile. One thing led to another when he got home and she said she was calling her parents in Opelousas and telling them that she and we children were going to live with them. Dad said she couldn't use the phone and bent down in the living room to disconnect it. While this was going on, Mom had moved all of the children with her by the front door except for me. Dad was between me and the front door. He said, "If you take one more step, I'll break your damn jaw!"

Mom said, "Come on, Dale!"

I stood there frozen. I knew that he meant every word he said. The argument went on for a long while and finally subsided. I had bad dreams for a long time after that.

I was afraid of suffocating. In the wintertime, I used to get in the bed, cover my head with the quilt, and curl up in a ball to go to sleep. During the night, I would get caught up in the quilt and couldn't find a way to get my head out in the open. I was terrified.

I was afraid of Pop-Pop and Mom-Mom's house. I thought that something evil lived in that house and maybe it was the devil. As I stated earlier, the house was dark with the shades pulled down tight and the furniture was black. It always seemed dirty and had a distinct odor to it. I did not trust Mom-Mom. I got goosebumps most of the time when I was near her. I found it very difficult to sleep in that house.

A fear that many children who are raised Catholic have is the fear of the devil. I certainly was no exception. The priests and the teachers scared us with stories about what the devil could do and how we could end up in hell with him. There were never the loving stories of what joy could come to our lives by loving Jesus and holding to His teachings. Most of the sermons came from the Old Testament and provided gloom and doom that could ruin any beautiful day. At one point in my childhood, I became afraid to go inside the church. They used incense in some of the services and had ominous-looking objects everywhere. The way the priests dressed for the mass seemed odd to me and I felt uncomfortable around it. There was an echo in the church because the ceiling was so high and I was afraid of that sound too. I felt the same evil there at times as I had in Mom-Mom's house.

This one may be hard for you to understand, but I was afraid of telling the truth. I mentioned earlier that all of my parents' children were afraid of telling the truth at times. Dad would want to find an excuse to beat one of us so he would manufacture a situation where he had supposedly told us to do or not to do something. I would do or not do the very thing he had manufactured. He would stand me in front of him while he was sitting down and drill me about it. Dad would repeatedly say, "Didn't I tell you not to...?"

My response was, "No sir!"

This would go on back and forth for a few minutes. I was telling him the truth, but that isn't what he wanted to hear. Once I realized that telling the truth was just making him angrier and that I was going to get beat no matter what, I just told him what he wanted to hear. I got used to telling him lies because telling the truth brought on a beating. Either way I went, the result was going to be the same. It was easier and quicker to tell the lie and get the beating over with.

Those were my fears, with the biggest one being killed by my parents. One day before I had started school, Mom had swept and was still in the process of mopping the dining room. She had poured some milk for Mike, and told him to stay in the kitchen with it. He didn't. She was in the dining room and so was I and the floor was still wet. We had a large dining room table and there was a large cut-crystal bowl in the center of it that Mom used for a centerpiece. Mike was standing north of me with his milk and spilled some of it on her freshly mopped floor. She went into a rage and began yelling and calling us names. She reached over, grabbed the bowl (that probably weighed 15 to 20 pounds), threw it at us, and shattered it into a thousand pieces against the wall. When I saw it coming, I grabbed Mike, threw him to the floor, and covered him with my body. Glass was all over me, but none reached Mike. I think her outburst scared her because she stood still for a couple of minutes before getting the broom. She never checked to see if we were alright nor did she help get the glass off of me. When my older siblings got home, Helen, Bubba, and Larry got the glass off of me.

About a week before I started the first grade, my parents went shopping and bought me two pairs of jeans, two shirts, a gray hooded jacket, a yellow rain jacket and hat, shoes, rain boots, color crayons, and a book satchel. I was all excited because I was a big boy and was going to school like the other big boys and girls. The excitement faded the first day of school.

My sister Helen took me to my class and left me there. Class had already started so all I saw was a bunch of kids that I didn't know sitting in a room that I didn't know with a woman I didn't know. I was scared out of my wits and ran for the door crying and yelling for Helen. Mrs. Black grabbed me roughly by the arm and put me at a desk. I cried all that day and all day she got onto me and told me to stop crying. She did try to console me once or twice, but quickly gave up. The next few days were the same. Finally, one day when everyone was going back inside from recess, I decided to not go in. The principal found me and brought me back in. When I got home I got a beating from my mom and another one when my dad got home. From that time forward, I stopped crying and started learning. I made straight As. The thing that my parents didn't understand was that they made me distrustful and afraid of all adults. Anyway, when they had open house to show off the kid's school work, Mrs. Black told them how well I had adjusted and what good grades I was making. She actually hugged me. I made something evil out of my relationship with her, though. You're probably thinking that it is impossible for a six-year-old to think about sexual immorality, but you are wrong.

My two older brothers began teaching me about sex when I was in the first grade. We would be sitting at the kitchen table doing our catechism lessons and they would begin telling me what would have happened if Adam had not sinned. They said that there would never have been a need for people to wear clothing. This meant that men would always be seen naked by women and vice versa. At that point, things got very vulgar. So, when Mrs. Black wore anything the least bit revealing, my mind began to wander. It didn't help that Mr. Lewis, our school principal, would come by our classroom several times a week, stand outside the doorway and flirt with her. She flirted back. Sometimes they would be at the door for as long as what seemed to be about thirty minutes. The first grade also taught me how poor children were treated differently than the rich kids. They made fun of the haircuts that I received. My dad cut our hair himself and he pretty much cut it all off once summers came. I didn't have a barber cut my hair until I was in the eighth grade.

When I got to the second grade, I had a very old teacher, but she had two student teachers the first half of the school year and two more the second half of the year. The first half, we had a very beautiful dark-haired student teacher named Miss Owens. One day when she had us doing some work, a classmate asked her if she was married. She told him she wasn't and he told her that he wasn't either. The whole class laughed, but I was angry. I had already had thoughts about her and she was mine. The second half of the school year Miss Green became our student teacher. Miss Green was a tall dishwater blonde with green eyes. She had been Miss Louisiana. Every boy in the class went crazy over her. Unfortunately, I began having the kinds of dreams that little boys in the second grade should never have. They eventually stopped, though, because of an incident about taking turns and one about a pencil.

Mrs. Camp put the same number of desks in each row. This way, each student on each row would be in charge of taking up the books and distributing the books. If a student was absent on their day, the one who sat behind them got to do this for two days; the absent student's day and their own. However, if the one that was absent was the fourth one in the row and had already had their turn and the fifth child had already had their turn, it didn't matter. It was still the sixth child's turn on his day just like the sixth seat of every other row. I was the sixth child so the day had come for the sixth child on each row to take up the books. Joey Coleman's mother was the sixth grade teacher that taught the "gifted" class. Her husband owned his own company and it had made them very wealthy. All the teachers at the school made a fuss over Joey. On this particular day, the fourth child was absent and Joey was the seventh child in our row. He sat behind me.

When Miss Green called for the books to be taken up, Joey got up and started taking them up. I also stood up and told him it was my day. She saw us arguing and asked what was going on. Joey explained that since one child was absent, he was the sixth child. I explained that I was in the sixth seat and hadn't had my day and this was my day to do it. She told me to sit down and told Joey to take up the books. I was very hurt and I cried as quietly as I could.

My dad used to bring cases containing boxes of Wallace number two pencils home from work. They gave them to him for free. Each box contained twenty pencils. This is the only kind of pencil I ever used in school. One day, Joey didn't have a pencil so he took mine off of my desk. I told him to give it back. Miss Green asked what was going on and Joey told her the story, but it was a lie. Recess was starting and she made us stay in the classroom during recess. She gave us time to work it out on our own, but Joey insisted in lying. When she came back, he persisted. I explained that my dad brought those pencils home to us, but she believed Joey instead. I reached down into my desk and brought up two more pencils just like it and showed them to her. It didn't matter. In her eyes, Joey was telling the truth and got to keep my pencil. I was made to stand in the corner of the front of the room. This way all the children could see me and I would be humiliated. Miss Green was out, as far as I was concerned.

The second grade is also where I met the boy who would be my best friend all the way through high school graduation. His name was John. John lived just a couple of miles from us, but in a VERY nice home with nice furniture and a lot of food. His dad was a fire chief. Anytime I went to play there, his mom always had an after school treat waiting on us. This is important because I experienced many foods that I would have otherwise not tasted until much later in life. What is most important is the fact that their family laughed and loved. If John did something he shouldn't have, he was punished, but not in the same way I was. They grounded him or took away privileges. He was funny too. If his parents were angry at him, he would say something that was so funny that they soon got over being angry.

The most important thing that John's family taught me was the love of Jesus Christ. They were Southern Baptist. John and his parents used to tell me about what went on at their church and what was being taught there. I didn't hear about how great it was to be a Baptist, but rather how great it was to have the love of Jesus Christ. From this point on, I knew that there was a better life for me somewhere and it would happen sometime. I just didn't know how or when. I asked to go to church with John but Mom wouldn't allow it. As I mentioned before, if you were not Catholic, according to my mom and the Catholic Church, you were going to hell. Just stepping into a different denomination would send you to hell. As a seven-year-old child, I could not imagine that people who lived with so much love between them would go to hell. However, I did understand that parents who abused their children could go to hell.

I mentioned earlier that I was a quiet child. I was quiet at home but, because of hanging out with John, I came out of my shell as long as I was at school and began to make a lot of friends. Some children made fun of my harelip and/or our poverty, but most of them liked me. I began to be funny at school too. The little girls began to notice me once I was in the fifth grade. This was bad. They began to talk about how cute I was and I had my first girlfriend that year. She, too, lived just a mile or two from me. I would go to John's house and we would walk to hers.

By the time I was in the sixth grade, Dad had become a Roman Catholic and he had finished his education. There were not as many beatings, but I really began to experience discrimination. It is important to note that I survived beatings that could have very well killed me. Surviving "the beating years" was my third chance at life. The discrimination wasn't so much from the teachers now, but it was from my own parents. I saved the little allowance money I began getting from my parents and I found coke bottles on the side of the road. At that time, a person could redeem those bottles for money. I searched the ditches constantly looking for bottles. Ban-Lon shirts for boys had become very popular. I wanted to be like the other kids so I saved enough to buy one. I know I had enough money because my brother Mike and I looked at the shirts anytime we were in a clothing store.

One day, Mom and my sisters went to town so I gave my mom the money and asked her to buy me a red one. Mike also went with her. When they came back, Mom handed me my red shirt and handed Mike a green and white one. I expected to get my money back from her since she had spent the same money on Mike. I knew Mike hadn't saved any money. He spent his on candy every time he got some. This didn't happen.

It seemed that every time that Dad or Mom went shopping downtown, they bought somebody something. Except for me. Tears are beginning to flow as I write these words. Remembering all the ways that I was neglected and abused is the worst experience of my life. I just don't understand why it had to happen to me. I experienced this all the way to my parents' deaths and still experience it after they are gone.

I have very crooked teeth. My brothers and sisters and some kids at school made fun of me and the siblings still talk about my teeth. I asked my dad if I could go to the dentist about it, but he said no. Really, my parents didn't take any of us, except Karen as far as I know. Even at that, I only remember them taking her once. My parents were first told that I needed glasses when I was in the fifth grade. A lady from the school board sat in on our class one day and came back the next day. When she did, I was called up to go with her. She took me to have my eyes examined and the amblyopia was discovered. My parents were told, but they didn't do anything about it. When I was in the sixth grade, the school was still telling them about it. Finally, I guess they got tired of it and took me to Dr. Flynn. Dad sat in the examination room while this was going on. Every time I couldn't read something, he would tell me to tell Dr. Flynn the truth. Dr. Flynn told him that he was absolutely certain that I was telling the truth and explained to him what amblyopia was. My left eyelid, as he explained, should have never been able to stay opened. This is what happens with most amblyopia patients. He gave my dad a prescription and sent us next door to get fitted for glasses. Once I got them, my siblings had one more thing to make fun of me for. They called me "four eyes" and threw other insults at me. It made me want to stop wearing them.

It was also in the sixth grade when I really started noticing the girls who were already developing as women. There was one in particular and I would touch or rub up against on purpose, but would swear it was an accident. This is the year that I discovered self-abuse. It was horrible. I went to confession at the church and the priest told me that he didn't think I could ever stop now that I had discovered it.

This is also the year that I began playing drums. When I was in the fifth grade, I asked my parents if I could join the band and learn how to play drums. After all, they had let my sister Karen join the band to learn how to play the clarinet and even bought her one. All I was asking for was a pair of drumsticks but they said we couldn't afford it. Once I began, I became not just good, but VERY good! The boys at school loved watching me play.

In the seventh grade, we got a new band director and I want everyone to know that he was prejudiced against poor children. He blamed me for every bad thing that happened and treated me like dirt. In turn, some of the other students began to do the same.

The next school year, I went to school with a lot of new clothes and with more self-confidence than I had ever had before. My two younger brothers and I had worked all summer at the church so we bought our own clothes. This time we could buy what we wanted instead of what my dad thought we ought to have. The guys in Mike's class told him that he and I were the best dressed guys in school. It was true. I became very popular in the eighth grade. I was funny, talented, dressed well, I was smart in school, athletic, and I had started wearing my hair like the Beatles and the Rolling Stones.

At thirteen years of age, I had sex for the first time. The girl was nineteen. This came about because there was a new pizza restaurant across from the university. My friend John, his cousin Russ, another friend of ours, and I went there to have lunch. Students from the beauty school in the same area were having lunch there too. I noticed this beautiful student with long, straight, black hair and blue eyes staring at me. Her white uniform was pulled up high on her legs and she was moving them back and forth. I finally had enough of the staring so I went to the table to pass her by and put my hand on her shoulder as I did so. I went to the bathroom and tried to calm down. Went I went back by her she said, "Here baby," and handed me her name, phone number, and address.

The next day while I was at John's house, I told him I had to leave him for a little while, but I would be back in a couple of hours. By this time, his parents had separated and he was living down the street from the university. I knocked on her door and she let me in. I thought I was just going to kiss her but she proved me wrong. She could have gone to jail for this. I did know that I could not tell anyone that this had happened and I never told anyone in school whenever I had sex with a girl. Girls, I figured, had it rougher than boys. Boys could have sex and they were considered "studs." If girls did the same thing, they were considered "whores."

Anyway, I knew that if I told anyone the name of any girl that I slept with, as was their habit, they would ask her out and I would never see her again. She finally broke things off when she met some guy about her age. It had gone on for five months. I went to John's house and was pretty much bummed out. For that reason, I didn't want another girlfriend in the eighth grade. That isn't the only reason, though. I was so popular that I felt that if I tied myself down to one girl, I wouldn't be able to flirt with the others. At my eighth grade graduation ceremony, all the girls decided to snub me because of this.

That same year, at age fourteen, I discovered that I could sing. John lived next door to some guys who were in a very popular band. They eventually got a record contract. At this time, the members were anywhere from twenty to twenty-six years of age. I went to see John on a Saturday night, but he wasn't home. Don, the band's leader met me in John's yard and asked what I was doing that night. I told him nothing. He was looking for John because the drummer had been in an accident and they were playing at the Saddle 'n' Spur that night. This was the most popular rock night club in Monroe, and Tommy Williams, the owner, was very particular on who he allowed to play there. He was a musician too. When we got there, he looked at me and said, "Who the @#%* is this?" Don explained the situation to him, but they both knew that Tommy would get in trouble if the police came in. They decided to remove the light bulbs over the drums. Don got a black grease pencil and made a mustache on my lip. We all hoped this would work.

I was very nervous so one of the guys gave me some rum and water. I wasn't nervous anymore. On one of the mellow songs we were playing, I was singing along and the bass player heard me. This led to more than what I expected. At the end of the night, Don told me to come to his house on Monday. I went and he told me what the bass player said. He had me sing some of the songs instead of the lead singer. The guy was very angry. He and Don had strong words and Don apologized to me and sent me home. He did, however, have me come over every now and then and he gave my name and number to other bands.

I formed a couple of bands myself and ended up being a professional musician without my parents knowing about it. I knew that my dad wouldn't allow me to do it. My junior year in high school, the school was having a "Battle of the Bands" and one of the teachers blackmailed me into playing. My brother Mike, being the brown-nose and tattle-tale he was, told my parents before I got home. There was silence in the whole house when I walked in. No one said a word for about ten minutes. This was unusual and I was concerned. Then, Dad told me that Mike told him that we had played and that we were very good. He said that anytime we needed a place to practice, we could do it in his house. By that time he had finished the addition to the house that included a living room the size of Texas.

Instead, I was practicing and playing behind everyone's back and making a lot of money. I never told anyone in my family. I played off and on professionally until I was twenty-seven years of age. I was in bands that opened for Jefferson Airplane, the Doors, America, Chicago, and others.

My favorite guitarist to open for was Jorma Kaukenen of the Airplane. In fact, I still communicate with Jorma. I became friends toward the end with Dan Peek of America and Gene Cotton. These guys were Christians and while Dan stopped playing rock for that reason, Gene didn't want his children to grow up without him. Gene had top ten hits one after the other when he left Wooden Nickel and went to Electra Asylum. They were upset that he didn't want this anymore. I was tired of the drugs and the lifestyle rock dictated. I was just tired, really.

Music made me more popular my junior and senior year in high school. I had beautiful girlfriends, but I dated a lot of people. I got, somehow, a bad reputation and it was understood that any girl who went out with me was going to get one as well. For this reason, the popular girls that I dated (with one exception) didn't want anyone to know that they had gone out with me. I honored their wishes and hope that they have changed their minds at their present age.

My senior year in high school I was going steady with a girl from another school. Her dad played for Ace Cannon. She didn't sleep with me at first so I had to make other arrangements. A redhead from California moved to Monroe and was in my math class. She and I hit it off pretty quickly. On her sixteenth birthday, she told me that she had never been kissed. I took her out that night and took her virginity. She was in love. The girl was living with her mother who was on welfare and was a prostitute on the side. She didn't tell me that, but other people did. They told me where she hung out and I saw her there. The girl told me that if she ever got pregnant, she wouldn't want me to marry her, she would never tell me, and that she would go where I would never find her. Once I started sleeping with my girlfriend, I never stopped seeing her. Her best friend wasn't a student at the school but came to tell me that she thought that the girl was pregnant. One morning when I was at school I learned that she had dropped out. She came to the school between classes and confirmed it. Later that day, there was a note taped inside my locker that said, "I told you so!"

I cared about her. In fact, I had begun to care more for her than the other girl. After school, I went to her house and her mother told me that she had packed up and left and she didn't know where she was going. She tried to get the police to track her down, but they were never able to. I searched on my own for about a year and gave up. I traveled as far as New Orleans because I knew she had a sister there, but I never found her. My girlfriend and I broke up and her family moved to Memphis.

After high school, I went to college at Northeast Louisiana University and majored in accounting. I still played music, and worked a number of jobs. In fact, this is a good time to let you know that the abuse and neglect I experienced at home made me not want to get close to people and led me to mistake other things for love. During my lifetime, I have held eighty-three jobs. I didn't get fired. I just didn't want to work there anymore. Some of my jobs included retail and restaurant management, bag boy in a grocery store, painter, carpenter, salesman, and accountant. Also during my lifetime, I have slept with two hundred and ninety-one females. I didn't care how old they were or if they were married or not. I just didn't want them to be ugly.

While I was at Northeast, I met a girl named Sharon. She was the first Christian girl I had dated. I had dated a couple who had professed to be Christian, but she lived it. It had a profound impact on my life. I started going to church with her and she with me. This was a very unselfish relationship. I did for her and she did for me without requiring anything in return from one another. I was still drinking and drugging, but stopped for a short time after meeting her. Her parents didn't approve of me. They had been married through an arrangement and mentioned it frequently to their children. Sharon broke up with me one day while we sat in the Student Union Building. She explained that her parents were putting pressure on her to break it off. She stood up for me until finally she told her parents to pick someone for her. You see, we had become engaged. They told her that it wasn't necessary and she could pick anyone she wanted as long as it wasn't me. I had even faked becoming a Christian just to be accepted by them. I'm not sure why, though. While they made sure their children went to church every Sunday, they didn't bother to go themselves. The breakup caused me to do drugs and drink constantly for a few months. The pain of losing her was the worst I'd experienced.

I dated a few people after that, but always found an excuse to take them home early. One rich girl from Bastrop, Louisiana got married soon after I stopped dating her. The rumor was that she was pregnant by me, but the guy married her because her family was wealthy. While I didn't have sex with Sharon, I did with all these girls. After it was over, I wanted to go home. I almost married one of them just to hurt Sharon for something she didn't do, but God intervened in that situation. He allowed me to see that this girl was sick in the head and the marriage would have been disastrous.

My brother Mike introduced me to a girl named Becky, her sister, and her next door neighbor while he was working at 7-Eleven. He told me that she wanted to go out with me so I explained that I drank a lot and tended to be someone you couldn't count on. She didn't care. I dated her for about a year and in that time we broke up repeatedly. I eventually said that I thought that I was a Christian and was baptized in her church (Southern Baptist like Sharon). The night before that happened, I was lying in bed hearing in my mind all the sermons that Sharon's pastor and Becky's pastor had given. I stayed awake all night, fell asleep about five o'clock, woke up at seven o'clock, and felt better than I had in years. I got up from bed and poured all the alcohol down the drain and flushed all the drugs down the toilet. This was the beginning of life number four. Becky ended up pregnant and we got married. I was accepted easily by her whole extended family.

We bought a mobile home, but sold it after about eight months and moved to Alexandria, Louisiana where I attended college to become a minister. It was there in Alexandria that I had a direct encounter with Satan. I came home one night and felt that something evil was in my house. I looked up at the head of the stairs and there was a cloud-like figure. I was afraid so I closed the door and tried again. It was still there, but as I moved closer, it moved away and eventually disappeared. Remember, I had seen this previously when my grandmother Mom-Mom passed away. I was licensed by Becky's church and preached. Yet, I still had a roaming eye and so did she. My grades were not what they should have been because I was working fifty-one hours a week, taking eighteen hours in school, and trying to take care of a family. We ended up moving back to Monroe and we bought a house. Our daughter was not quite one when we moved to Alexandria and she wasn't quite two when we moved away.

Becky went to work at an auto parts store and the guys thought she was hot. They all hit on her. She worked with a manager named Mike, who was also married, yet he asked her out. She made the mistake of telling my best friend's wife that she would go out with him if she knew she wouldn't get caught. Becky told me that she liked getting attention from other men. She got fired from that job and several other jobs. She had a smart mouth and it always got her into trouble.

Our next door neighbor's sister came to visit one time. She and Becky had become friends and we were always in and out of each other's houses. The sister sat on our sofa looking at a yearbook and we ended up kissing while Becky was in the kitchen cooking. Becky saw it, but didn't say anything right away. The girl looked like Hee-Haw's Barbie Benton. Becky and I split. No one thought we would because I loved my little girl so much. She was her daddy's girl. When she was first born, I would drive as fast as I could to get home and play with her. She always wanted me to read to her because I would use different voices for each character. Becky and everyone else said I was a good daddy. I missed that girl. I realized what I had done was wrong and tried to patch things up. By this time Becky was going out with a different guy every night. She even put Jennifer to bed early to fall asleep and then locked her up in the house while Becky went out. When I was over there to pick her up to visit with me one day, the neighbor called me over and told me to get that baby out of that house and soon. She and her sisters told me what was happening. Becky's sister told my parents what was happening. I should have known this because one day when Jennifer was staying with me, she cried when I told her that I had to go to the store. She said, "You'll be back?"

I said, "Jennifer, you're going with me!"

I guess I was slow and didn't realize that she was hinting that her mother was leaving her alone in the house at night. I wish I had been more alert. We were about to get her out when my brother Larry, meaning to do good, told the guy that had moved in with Becky that he had a third degree black belt in karate and he was coming over to hurt him. The guy found out that it was true and got himself out of there. We didn't get my daughter out.

I dated and eventually moved in with the neighbor's sister, but it was short-lived. She had a high-pitched voice and would whine all the time. She would hang on my arm and say, "Dale! Dale!" I got sick of it. I was in an auto accident that nearly cost me my life and never moved back in with the girl. Surviving that accident gave me life number five. By this time the divorce was settled and I got to keep the car, the house, and everything in it.

I started living with a girl from Sterlington, Louisiana. We moved into a mobile home in West Monroe. She was a sweet girl and one of the most beautiful I dated. However, she was a girl who could not say no to anyone. She cheated on me with a guy that she had dated previously. Two friends of hers didn't like me and told her that the guy was in town. He came to where we were and didn't stay but for a minute. She made up a story to get away from me, realizing she was taking a risk. A month before she told friends of ours that she knew that if she ever cheated on me I would not take her back. Still, she stayed out all night with him. I tried to make it work when she came home, but things were not the same. The guy knew she was in love with me and even told her to work it out with me. It was too bad we couldn't get past it because Jennifer was crazy about her.

I moved away to Jackson, Mississippi for a while, but came back before even a whole year was over. When I got back, I was arrested for not paying child support. I stopped paying it because Becky was spending the money on going out instead of spending it on Jennifer. Every time I went to see Jennifer, she had on clothes that were either dirty, shabby, or too small on her. I bought her some clothes but I finally realized that I was paying child support to take care of that.

I went to work at a couple of places, including my baby brother's company, but I was restless. While working for a company that transferred me to Ruston, Louisiana I started going back to church. When people realized I was that drug-dealing Dale Douglas, revival broke out, not only in that church (they had just finished building on because things were beginning to happen there), but most of Northeast Louisiana. They knew me.

I was invited to speak at churches all over the state and

I was enjoying it. Then, my company transferred me to Winnsboro, Louisiana. My pastor told me that it was too soon for me to be leaving. I had not grown enough and everyone wanted to help me with that. The Christian community reached out to me in a way that I had never seen before. Still, I had to move.

As soon as I got to Winnsboro, the pastors of the two Southern Baptist churches there paid me a visit trying to get me to join their churches. I ended up in the one with the least amount of money. The people were real there. They allowed me to be active in the choir and to give my testimony to each group. They treated me like family. It was here that I had another encounter with Satan. I drove up to my house and felt evil was waiting inside. Once I stepped in, I really felt a strong evil presence. This was the first time that I turned the lights on to sleep. As I was trying to sleep, the devil grabbed my wrists and began pulling on me. I yelled out, "No! No!" and asked God to help me. He released me.

I got fired from my job because the girl that was my assistant wanted my job. She wanted it when her last boss left, but they transferred me instead. I went to work for a local painter because I didn't want to leave Winnsboro. God had other plans. The music evangelist Mark Tullos did a revival at church. The people there told him about me and he asked me to travel with him one day to visit the schools. I did go with him and gave my testimony in each one. In every school we went to, kids gave their hearts to Christ. If we had stayed long enough to hear each child that had come forward in each school, we would have had to be there for months. I cried in the car as we headed back to the church and asked if God could use somebody like me.

He said, "Brother! He already is!" He then told me that he was going to knock on a few doors and see where they might lead. They led to the Acadian Baptist Center in Eunice,

Louisiana and Brother Joe Backus.

This was a Baptist Camp with an Olympic swimming pool, large cafeteria, and plenty of wide open space. I loved being there. During the week we would mow the lawn and take care of whatever maintenance we needed to. On weekends, we had churches come with their own programs or taking part in the ones we prepared for them. Brother Joe had me share my testimony quite often and he used me as the music director on weekends. I led hundreds of young people to the Lord there. Then one day, Tom Dodge, the pastor of First Baptist Church of Sunset, Louisiana, came to see Brother Joe. Brother Joe sent Ray (his son-in-law) to take me to his office. When I got there he introduced me to Tom and told me that Tom wanted me to be youth director at his church on Wednesday nights and weekends. Brother Joe told him what to pay me and recommended me highly. In just one month, we had the top youth group in our association. The kids came out of the woodworks to be in the group. While I was there, I met a girl from Colorado. She was separated from her husband and living with her in-laws. The in-laws encouraged her to go out with me and she did. We ended up sleeping together and moved in together in Alexandria, Louisiana. Obviously I left the camp and the church.

We were only in Alexandria a short time before we went to Colorado. Her parents let us stay with them for a month and then we got our own place. These people did not go to church. I ended up working for them in their restaurant and became the manager. She had a little girl who lived with us. This was not a pretty child, but she was a charmer. I loved that kid. At some point, we split up and I went to work at another restaurant. Her little girl still called me, "Daddy" and people said that I may not have been her father, but I was absolutely her daddy. I finally moved back to Louisiana and stayed with Uncle Jack for a month before getting my own place. I got work right away so it didn't take long.

A girl that had been a friend of mine when I was dating the girl from Sterlington called me because her mother knew where I was working. She knew I had been living in Colorado and wanted to see me. I went to her house and she told me she had married, but was separated from her husband. We talked for a couple of hours and ended up sleeping together. She told me she loved me. She called me from her mother's house the next day. Her mother told her that she could tell that there was something special between us and I guess there was.

I met and started seeing another girl because I didn't know what was going to happen between this friend and her husband. I was seeing both of them. The other girl was separated from her husband and had a child. Eventually, my friend went back to her husband. Her mother told me that she told her it was a mistake, but she wanted to be successful at marriage since her mother had failed at it several times.

The other girl ended up being psychotic. She loved hard and hated hard. We moved in together and this was a big mistake. She was insanely jealous. If I came home just ten minutes later than what she thought I should have, she would scream at me and beat on me. She would slap my face, scratch me with her fingernails, and hit me. I had nightmares brought on by her behavior. There was a deep feeling of the presence of evil being around her. In fact, in living with her, I had my next encounter with Satan. We were asleep and I fell into that realm type of sleep. Again, the devil grabbed me by my wrists and told me that I was going to hell with him. The girl woke me up because apparently I was yelling for help in my sleep. When I would go out to my car each morning to go to work I would find notes on the windshield from my neighbors asking if I was OK and if I needed help. It was humiliating. I realized that I was being abused emotionally, mentally, verbally, and physically all over again. I was going to leave her, but she got pregnant. The birth of our son did not fix our problems. Everyone thought we were married, including our parents. We split up and I was relieved. Then, I had a heart attack as I was going down the stairs outside of my new apartment. This was brought on by all the stress this maniac was causing me. The neighbors saw me and got me to the hospital. God gave me still another chance at life.

I was ordered to pay child support, but she wouldn't allow me to see my son unless she supervised it herself. This made me very uncomfortable. When I would debate the arrangement, she told me that I had to do whatever she wanted because she held all the cards. She also told me that I would never be free of her and that she would always control me. I proved her wrong.

After making all kinds of efforts to resolve the visiting rights, I did the only thing left to get from out of her control. I gave up the right to my son. This was a shock to everyone and she was furious. The woman wasn't angry about not receiving the money. She was angry because she would no longer be able to control me. My meddling sister, Helen, told everyone that I did this because I didn't want to pay child support. I guess no one knew how afraid I was of her. She took him to my parent's house and showed them the letter. They didn't say much because she had not allowed them to see my son either. My parents had kept him and her son while she worked to help her with her finances. She stopped bringing him there a couple of years before I sent the letter so he didn't even know that they were his grandparents. She had hoped that they would talk me out of it, but they understood.

I moved to Shreveport and married a Ralph Lauren model. I didn't know her very long, but she could drink more than any man I ever saw. This is the first time I stopped going to church, but it was only for a few weeks. She had a son and a daughter and had been married to a wealthy man. Her overweight, detestable next door neighbor thought he was a player and he was obsessed with her. The day that we got married he called her and asked if she had gone through with it. When she told him she had, he broke down and cried. Every day he would sneak love notes to her, so I decided I should have a talk with him. When I confronted him, he told me that he wasn't after my wife because he had all kinds of women. We all knew that was a lie. Because I had stopped going to church, my life with her was crumbling day by day and we eventually split. When I left, I left all my belongings as well. It wasn't worth it. I just wanted out.

I ran into a girl I had known in high school about this time and ended up moving in with her. I didn't know that she had been sexually abused by her father for years before getting out on her own. She had married and had a son but that still didn't stop him from making sexual advances toward her. Obviously, by the time I met her she had been divorced for several years, but didn't have custody of her son. She was bi-polar so I never knew what to expect when she came home or when I came home. We split up quickly.

I joined the singles group at First Baptist Church in West Monroe, Louisiana and met a lady who had been separated a short time. She had two daughters. We began seeing each other and the kids loved me. She told me that I was like a toy to them. We got married and went to church every Sunday. I kept changing jobs pretty quickly and finally decided to move to Texas. She and the kids came to see me and I went back to see them. One time I went back to see them and she told me that we were not married. It seems that the lady I was married to in Shreveport had not divorced me like she said she had. So, I had to divorce her instead. Still, this lady did not want to move to Texas and leave a house that was almost paid for. Who could blame her? Besides, I was cheating on her in Texas anyway and she suspected it.

After being in Texas about a year, I met and married another lady. I had met her in church. She had terminal cancer, but I didn't care. We bought a house together. Her kids were a problem. They were all pretty much grown and they were always in trouble. They stole from her and they stole from me. One of them smoked marijuana in the house and another one sneaked a girl in the house to spend the night with him. All they did was act disrespectfully toward me and her. I had another heart attack because of the stress I was experiencing, but I got to the hospital in plenty of time. God gave me another life.

One of the children borrowed her car, didn't put gas in it, left it out on a country road, and someone broke into it. They took the radio, broke out the windows, and trashed the whole interior. Another son asked to borrow her car, stole her credit card, charged over $300 on it, shoplifted, broke into cars, totaled her car, and was arrested over and over again. We had no peace in that house. Her children knew she was dying, but they didn't care. In the meantime, she was cheating on me. She told me that she had cheated on her first husband with a married minister from a mega-church in the Dallas/Ft. Worth area. I took all I could and got out. We had gone to a marriage counselor, but she refused to go back after he told her that she was married to her children instead of me. I divorced her. She passed away shortly after that, but before she died, she spread all kinds of lies about me at our church. Almost everyone that worked there from the pastor on down helped her spread her lies. She never mentioned how her children abused both herself and me, though. Her first husband warned me that I would encounter this and he was correct.

I lived alone then for a couple of years and was still attending church. I dated a few people, but did not want to get into another relationship. A friend of mine wanted me to go with him to a singles event that his church was sponsoring. I said no about forty times, but he kept on until I said I would. My hair was completely silver, I had a deep suntan, and I was in probably the best shape of my life. Ladies were flirting like crazy and he continuously pointed this out to me. I wasn't interested in any of them. One Friday night I went to one of the events and ladies were flirting with me as usual, but I noticed a redhead with glasses sitting quietly with some other people. I noticed her because she was probably the only girl there who wasn't trying to impress the men.

I introduced myself to her and asked to dance. I danced with a lot of women that night, but I was only interested in her. She was not the pretty Barbie Doll type. She looked and acted conservatively. It was a great relief to me that she had never been married and especially that she did not have children. I left without getting her phone number.

A month later I was at another of those functions and saw her there. I explained to her that my friend and I looked through several phone books trying to find her phone number but never did. She then reached in her purse for pen and paper and gave it to me.

I called her about six or seven times before I could get a date with her. She wasn't putting me off. This was a girl with a lot of friends, so she was always doing something with one or some of them. Once I did get a date with her, we saw one another a lot. I was driving a sports car, had a very expensive apartment, was making serious money, dressed to the tens, and believed in going out to dinner only in the best restaurants. I sent her flowers a lot. This was an unpretentious relationship. I didn't make it a Disneyland

Romance. It is fair to say that I did not fall in love with her. I was determined to marry someone who was nothing like the other girls and women I had been with. She wasn't. Lynn has a learning disability, but I didn't care. Her morals were very much intact. We talked a lot and about everything. We went to church together and called one another every day. If we had an argument, I found that I was wrong after careful thought I would call her and apologize. I was treading new water. I had never done that before. I made a decision to love her. It was the best decision I ever made.

Lynn and I have been together for twenty years now. We bought a home and I did all the remodeling myself. While visiting my parents in Monroe one weekend, I told my dad that I was almost through remodeling the house. He laughed. I asked what he was laughing about and he said, "You will never be done remodeling your house." I thought he was saying that I didn't know what I was doing, but that wasn't it. He knew that I was a workaholic like him and I would continuously find things to change.

Lynn and I got involved with the community immediately. We went through the Citizens Police Academy and sponsored our neighborhood National Night Out for years. I even ran for mayor one year and came close to winning. During the election, my dad passed away. This unraveled me. He and I had become friends in my adult years and he was a kinder, gentler man. I grieved him enormously for three long years. I cried almost every day. After three years, a minister friend of mine said, "Dale, you have got to stop this! This is not what your dad wants. As much as he loves you, he does not want to come back here to you. He is with God and he could never be as happy as he is now here on earth."

We started a charity called "The H. E. Douglas, Sr. Memorial New Shoes for Little Feet Foundation" in order to provide new shoes for children whose families could not afford to buy them for them. If you recall, my dad had not had a new pair of shoes until he was sixteen years of age. His feet were in a mess when he passed away. The police and fire department, most of the local restaurants, many other businesses, our congressman in Washington, D.C., our state congressional leaders, some of the local churches, the local Boy Scouts, and the local government officials helped, sponsored, and contributed to it. The actual event to hand out the shoes was a Christmas Party at the police station training facility. We had receptacles for shoes and/or money spread throughout the city. Professional talent donated their time to entertain them. We made this the poor's special day one day a year. In 2005, this charity was recognized by the Congress of the United States as being one of the most important charities in Texas.

In 1998 we found out that I had stomach cancer. I did the treatments and lost my hair, but I was alive. We never worried about me surviving. We just knew I would. This is when I began reading through my Bible twice a year. My company threatened my job if I didn't come to work. The human resources vice president told me that they expected me to be at work unless I was dead. I called the owner of the company and told him what this guy told me. It is fair to note that I was providing the company with more profits than any of my counterparts. I was his boy. Within minutes the V. P. called me back and apologized. Once the doctors released me, I went to work elsewhere providing them with higher profits than any of my counterparts. God gave me still another life.

In 2000 the bottom fell out for us financially. We had to go to our savings to live. I got a job, but it wasn't a very good one. Lynn had gained weight, so she didn't have many clothes. Yet, she never complained. In 2005, we had been teaching Bible Study at our church and felt that the Lord was calling me back into the ministry. I talked to one of the ministers and he asked me to meet him in his office that Monday. We met and talked and he gave me something for thought. He gave me a long list of things to try and get done (this includes getting back in school and getting the money to get back in school) and told me that if I could get all of this done, it would verify that the Lord was calling me back. He also told me not to get discouraged because this would probably take from six months to a year to get done. The next day, I emailed him to let him know that it was all done. I started back to school to get a Christian studies degree. It took me two years to complete my bachelors, one to get my masters, and two to get my doctorate. I went straight through. I finished my B. A. S. with honors, had a 3.987 in my masters, and a 4.0 in my doctorate program.

I was working on staff at our church under the minister who I had spoken to while I was getting educated. I wasn't making much money, but I was leading many people to the Lord. Another church called me to work part time as an associate pastor, but neither of these jobs paid much. One day in 2006, I was sitting in my recliner reading one of my text books with the front door opened. Lynn had come home and walked up the sidewalk toward the house. I began to cry when I saw her. She was dressed so shabbily. I prayed that night that the Lord would help me get her some new clothes. On faith, I used our credit card to purchase $1,000 worth of clothes for her; praying that the Lord would provide the money to pay this off because I knew I couldn't do it with what we were getting paid.

Within three days, money was coming in and we ended up with all the money to get this paid off. It came from people from my school, people from church, her grandmother, and others. We never told anyone that we needed this.

In March of the next year, I had to give up the associate pastor's job. I was stretched too thin and I knew it. Now we were really hurting for money. Since I did all the cooking and we never got a chance to eat together, I came up with a plan. I would cook enough food for Lynn and I would just not eat. I would dirty a plate and put it in the sink or dishwasher to make her think I was eating. When I got really hungry, I would go to the Kroger near us and get something out of the dumpster. Sometimes I couldn't because they have a policy not to allow people to do that. An employee would be there watching so I would turn around.

In the fall of that year, I had to write a paper for a group of professors that I didn't know on why I deserved to get credit for classes through the adult learner program. I told them how I had been going to the dumpster and the rest of the story. In the meantime, the school sent me a bill and said I didn't have enough money to pay for school so I needed to send more. I didn't have any. I called financial aid and told the girl that I didn't have any money and I would just drop out. By this time the paper had been read by my professor over the adult learner class. She called someone who called someone else and so on. I received a call from Wesley in financial aid and he told me that he was sending me a check for over three thousand dollars. I told him that was great because now I could pay for my semester. He then told me that someone had taken care of that and the check was for me to take care of my family. I cried, of course and thanked God in prayer right away. From that point on, Dallas Baptist University made sure that they found money to pay my tuition and extra money to help us live a dignified life. My wife had no idea I was starving myself and eating out of a dumpster. She didn't find out until the end of the semester when she was snooping through my school work. She cried.

Shortly after that, in February of 2009, I was hit by an eighteen wheeler on I-75. He hit me and dragged me underneath his trailer for about five miles. The man was on his cell phone and had no idea I was there. He had driven into my lane because the high-five construction was confusing. He had never been here before. Cars were blowing their horns and waving at him, but he wasn't paying attention. While I was underneath him, an amber glow came into the car and a peace came over me. I said three things to myself: (1) I am going to die, (2) Lord, who is going to take care of Lynn, and (3) God help me. Just when I said that, the car broke loose, I spun around several times, and the car came to a stop up against the wall going the correct way and out of harm's way. When the driver got to me I was already out of the car. He looked at me, looked at the car, and then looked at me again. He asked, "How did you get out?" I looked at the car and said I didn't know. The car was crushed to the size of a love seat. When the police officers got there they did the same thing and I told them the same thing. Now I do know because there is no possible way I could have gotten out of that car on my own. Another life was given to me. This car, by the way, was given to us because one of our cars had stopped running and the other one was barely running. We sold both of them and only had this car a short time.

I preached at various churches in Texas and Louisiana in lieu of a call to be pastor. I actually sent out over two thousand resumes, but never got a pastor position. I believe the reason for this was discrimination against my age. When I applied for an education director's position at a local large church, almost every minister from Prestonwood (my home church) either sent letters, e-mails, or made phone calls to recommend me. Yet, I still didn't get the job. When I went for the interview, the guy took a look at me and told me that I didn't have enough experience. If that was true, why was I there interviewing in the first place? He discriminated against me because of my age. I would not say this if I didn't know that it was true. Every minister there was young and he hired a very young man with no experience to fill the position. I stopped sending resumes. I couldn't even get a job at Dallas Baptist University after spending tens of thousands of dollars there. My grades and the fact that I praised the school and promoted it to every potential student I could still didn't help me.

I finally finished school and, in the meantime, had been sending Lynn back to school. She will graduate in December of 2015 with a healthcare management degree. Her average will be honor student level. They do not give honors to adult learners. Remember, Lynn has a learning disability. Everyone told her she could not do this. Her high school teachers said she couldn't do this. Her mother told me that I was setting her up for failure. I believed she could do it. She is doing it. God is watching over Lynn.

I retired in 2014 before I was ready, but things worked out this way for a reason. I have been able to get things done around the house that needed doing for a long time. I began playing music again, but just as I was getting opportunities to play, I got arthritis in my hands. Lynn ran out of financial aid last year so I sold all of my guitars and equipment to make sure she got to finish. For the past few months, I have begun to starve myself again during the week without Lynn knowing it and eat only on weekends. This way Lynn is still able to eat. I have no regrets. She is so excited and ready to send invitations to everyone who told her she couldn't graduate.

Last year when I told her dad that she had run out of financial aid after getting so close to graduation, he said, "Well I'm sorry to hear it. That's too bad!" That is all he said. He didn't ask how he could help. He just didn't care. He had promised to help her if she needed it when she started eight years ago, but neither he nor Lynn's mother lifted a finger to help. Yet, to hear them talk, they are responsible for her success. I asked them to help with her class ring, but they said they had their own bills to pay. Just so that you will know, her father inherited a very large amount of money from his mother and has been spending it like there is no tomorrow. Yet, he can't do anything for his daughter. When I finished my masters, her mom said we should all go out to eat, so we did. When the bill came, her parents expected me to pay for everyone and I did. We couldn't afford it, but we did it anyway.

What I am trying to tell you is that Lynn was abused emotionally and verbally all her life. If it wasn't her parents, it was her teachers, fellow students, bosses, or coworkers. I have worked hard to make her realize that she is anything but stupid and instill some self-confidence in her. It hasn't worked all that well. But I will say, I have been asked by many people countless times how would I describe our marriage. I told them I could use one word: fun. It has been fun. Lynn and I have rarely ever argued. When we have, it has lasted no more than five minutes and we always make up. We love one another and we make sure that Christ is in the center of our marriage, no matter what happens.

The times that we have had money, we gave it away or we used it on our house. We strive to be generous on Christmas, birthdays, and giving other gifts, receiving little in return except from her family.

I renewed my relationship with my daughter about ten years ago. I showered her, her husband, and her children with expensive gifts. Then, she called us only when she needed or wanted money and we gave freely. One time, we found out she didn't need the money for what she told me. She and her two oldest daughters just wanted to go to a concert and the tickets were expensive. We didn't say anything. Another time, we sent money because she said it was an emergency, but we read on Facebook that she took her family out to eat with it.

When I retired, I called her and told her that I was on a fixed income and could no longer send money. She asked for it twice after that and I reiterated what I told her about my fixed income. She didn't call again, took me off as a parent on Facebook, hasn't called me to tell me Happy Father's Day, and has bashed me to everyone. She was just using me for the money. We never allowed money to go to our heads. Lynn calls me a tightwad, but I say I am just frugal. I tell her that she is a good spender. It works out.

You are probably appalled by what you have read about me and may not think that I am a Christian, but I know that I am because of the promises contained in the scriptures. I have put them all to the test and the results are always the same and for the better. The main problem that I face is learning to trust. Most of that was caused by the destruction of trust from abusive parents. My brothers and sisters destroyed my trust for them, too. They used to plan outings when Helen went to Monroe and they called everyone to go. They would tell one another not to call me and they didn't. Mom was mad at me so they had to be mad, too. However, I never missed church while I was on drugs or chasing women. Whenever I tried to get away from God, He brought me right back. Lynn and I know that our names are written in the Book of Life. We are Christians. I may have those times that I don't act too much like it, but I am. I didn't take care of my Christianity for a long time so I didn't mature like I should have. This isn't God's fault, but mine.

I stay away from my siblings because I do not want to be dysfunctional ever again. I love my Jesus and I keep a journal to write down His blessings each and every day. All the abuse and neglect that I went through is over and done. There have been brighter days and there are even brighter days ahead still. No one is going to have a perfect life, but no one can have any life without God period. Living without God is surviving life. It isn't living life. I choose to live it.

CHAPTER TEN

Putting it all Together

When I was a little boy, all little boys wanted a Tonka Truck for Christmas. They were made of metal, had bright, shiny, and flawless paint jobs, were sturdy and could stand up to just about anything, and, even though there were different models, they were still all Tonka. As soon as a boy received his truck, he would laugh and get giddy because he was so excited. The boy would show it to all of the kids that lived near him and told the kids at school all about it. Once it was in his possession, he and the truck were inseparable. For a while. Soon the newness wore off and the truck would get left out in the rain, heat, snow, and storms. The toy had to face the world alone. The little boy no longer cared about his truck and paid less and less attention to it, until he no longer touched it. The truck got a little rust on it. Then it got a lot of rust on it. Even the poorest of children didn't want it. No one ever asked the boy what happened to that Tonka Truck he was so proud of. They were not interested in it either.

As I have gone through life, I have come to realize that my sisters, brothers, and I were Tonka Trucks. We were all different, but we were all Tonka and all Tonka Trucks were made by the same maker with the idea that we would be resilient and last a very long time. Each of us was new at birth and our parents were excited. They were so excited that they told family, friends, neighbors, and others about us. They paid a lot of attention to us for a short time and then the newness wore off. We were neglected so we began to rust. When we began to rust, we were abused and thrown around and left for others to abuse as well. Because we were each different, we rusted in different ways and at different rates of time. Somewhere along the road, we saw other Tonkas being played with and cared for. They weren't left out in the elements. If they got wet, someone wiped them dry. If they got dirty, someone cleaned them. If their wheels came off, someone put them back on. We never knew until that time that Tonkas could be cared for like that. Why weren't we treated like that? We didn't think people could see that we had rust on us, but they could. They chose to ignore it and not to report it, but they saw it.

I often wondered as I walked through life why God brought me into this world. I, like the prophet Jeremiah, have said, "Cursed be the day on which I was born! The day when my mother bore me, let it not be blessed! Cursed be the man who brought the news to my father. 'A son is born to you,' making him glad. Let that man be like the cities that the Lord overthrew without pity; let him hear a cry in the morning and an alarm at noon, because he did not kill me in the womb; so my mother would have been my grave, and her womb forever great. Why did I come out from the womb to see toil and sorrow, and spend my days in shame?" (Jeremiah 21:14-18, ESV).

I have felt like Job: "Why did I not die at birth, come out from the womb and expire?" (Job 3:11, ESV).

God reminds me, though, "Has the potter no right over the clay?" (Romans 9:21). God made me in His image just as He has every man and woman on earth. Our lives have never been our own and never will be. We see the uncertainty on the future of our lives and the lives of others and feel that God does not treat us all equally. It is easy for children like my siblings and I to feel that God never cared about us and has never been watching over us. Then we are reminded, "For I know the plans I have for you, declares the Lord, plans for welfare and not for evil, to give you a future and a hope. Then you will call upon me and come and pray to me, and I will hear you. You will seek me and find me, when you seek me with all your heart I will be found by you, declares the Lord" (Jeremiah 29:11-14, ESV).

God never intended for any of us to go through what we went through. He never approved of the way we were treated, but He gave us His word that He had better plans for us and He would be there for us if we would just reach out to Him. Some of us reached out. Some of us didn't.

You see, we can either sit in our mess or we can get up and go forward. Jesus told His disciples in Luke 9:5 that wherever people do not receive you, when you leave, shake off the dust as a testimony against them (ESV). All of us who have been abused or neglected need to shake off the dust and get on with our lives. Some of us are strong enough to do that because we lean on God and His promises. Some of us have not sought out God and therefore have tried to shake off the dust, only to fail over and over again. The pain can go away, but only by the hand of God. "For everyone who calls on the name of the Lord will be saved" (Romans 10:13, ESV). God is waiting for those who will call on Jesus so that they can be His. This doesn't mean that the pain will go away instantly, but it does mean that Jesus will carry you through it.

The local church is a very good resource for getting to know God and getting the help that an adult who was abused as a child needs. Let me warn you though. The local church is made up of imperfect people. That includes imperfect ministers as well. Very few ministers are going to be as open and honest as I am about their own sins, so don't expect it. If you put too much hope on people instead of on God, you will be disappointed. Learn to forgive and ask God for guidance. The church is still a good place to start as long as you remember that you are imperfect, too. However, there are others and they are listed in the back of this book.

I know the pain that comes with abuse, but I also know the joy that can come from having Jesus lift me high on His shoulder and carry me through it all. Everyone can. Jesus is reaching His hand out right now. He is the only one who can remove the rust and restore you. Allow yourself to be touched by Him and find the rest and love you were meant to have. The world's ways will leave you rusting in the storm. But hear this: You were not made to be a rusting toy. God bless you.

RESOURCES

NATIONAL CHILD ABUSE HOTLINE: 1-800-4-A-CHILD (1-800-422-4453). Crisis Counselors are available 24/7

JOYFUL HEART FOUNDATION: 1-212.475.2026

SAFE HORIZON: 1-800-621-4673

CHILD WELFARE INFORMATION GATEWAY: 1-800-394-3366

NATIONAL ASSOCIATION OF ADULT SURVIVORS OF CHILD ABUSE: 1-323-552-6150

PARENTAL ALIENATION AWARENESS ORGANIZATION: 1-416-840-5654

NATIONAL ASSOCIATION FOR PEOPLE ABUSED IN CHILDHOOD: 0808-801-0331

THE DANDELION FOUNDATION: 1-406-952-0717

WINGS FOUNDATION: 1-303-238-4739

CONNECT WITH DR. DALE DOUGLAS:
www.DrDaleDouglas.com

CPSIA information can be obtained at www.ICGtesting.com
Printed in the USA
BVOW02s0315021115

425084BV00001B/75/P